"Collins's new greatest hits collection, *Sailing Alone Around the Room,* is certainly hospitable. There are brainy, observant, spit-shined moments on almost every page. . . . You finish [it] f... ...ate stampe...

man is Americ...' poet la...

clarity and appa...

"Collins uses o... ...he cadences of speech. They usua... ...then something strange happens. A rocket goes off, images ...st out like fireworks, and life's backyard becomes a magic kingdom. . . . Collins is often very funny—but more startling than the wit is the way his mind makes unexpected leaps and splices." — *The Boston Globe*

"Collins's new and selected poems shows how he attracts such a vast audience: by offering a pleasant tune sung in a pleasant way. . . . He is master of the everyday. . . . Collins reveals the unexpected within the ordinary. He peels back the surface of the humdrum to make the moment new." — *The Christian Science Monitor*

"Like a master jazz trumpeter, Collins takes quirky, imaginative leaps that are as stunning for their coherence as their originality. . . . Collins's popularity hinges on the accessibility of his poems and their mildly subversive quality. The vast majority are written in the first person, in the colloquial, richly perceptive tradition of William Carlos Williams. . . . So obviously a virtuoso, Billy Collins is sure to bring many new readers to poetry." — *The Washington Post Book World*

"To begin with, Collins is absolutely charming. He deserves every rose he's flung these days. . . . His poems are irresistible. Deceptively simple and gentle, they wrap their friendly arms around you, tell you a joke, pour you a drink and then usher you into a banquet of images and ideas." — Minneapolis *Star-Tribune*

"[Collins] writes out . . . one of the major poetic scripts of our time: the one that finds transcendence in the ordinary, and sings hymns to the banal. The most obvious thing to say about Collins's poetry is that it is funny, in an accessible and immediately familiar way. But his true poetic gift is something more than a sense of humor; it is a genuine, often debased, wit. . . . At its most powerful, this kind of wit is truly creative: if, as Emerson said, every word began life as a metaphor, wit resurrects the metaphor hiding in ordinary words."
—*The New Republic*

"Collins has reached into so many unexplored corners that he has elevated the mundane, not out of proportion to the world, but to a place where it seems to have always belonged."
—*The Miami Herald*

"Often, Collins will use the most mundane of subjects as a starting point for his work . . . but then he'll take the poem to somewhere strange, marvelous and emotionally resonant."
—*The Chicago Tribune*

"Because he is so accessible, there is a tendency to underrate Collins, but there is an intellectual challenge to most of his work."
—Cleveland *Plain Dealer*

"[Collins's] poetry insistently appeals to the mainstream. It brims with shared confidences, speaking softly and inviting the reader to come a little closer to the page. He does not write above or below his audience, but right at them. He engages us in intimate conversation."
—*The Dallas Morning News*

"The surface structure of these poems appears simplistic, but subtle changes in tone or gesture move the reader from the mundane to the sublime. . . . The results are accessible, but not trite, comical but not laughable, and well crafted but not overly flamboyant. . . . This volume belongs in every library."
—*Library Journal*

BILLY COLLINS is the author of six
collections of poetry, including
*Questions About Angels; The Art of
Drowning; Picnic, Lightning;* and, most
recently, *Nine Horses*. He is a
Distinguished Professor of English at
Lehman College of the City
University of New York. He was
appointed Poet Laureate of the
United States for 2001–2003.

SAILING ALONE AROUND THE ROOM

Sailing Alone
Around the Room

NEW AND
SELECTED POEMS

Billy Collins

RANDOM HOUSE TRADE PAPERBACKS

NEW YORK

Poems from *Picnic, Lightning,* by Billy Collins, ©1998, are reprinted by
permission of the University of Pittsburgh Press. Poems from *The Art
of Drowning,* by Billy Collins, ©1995, are reprinted by permission of
the University of Pittsburgh Press. Poems from *Questions About Angels,*
by Billy Collins, ©1991, are reprinted by permission of the University
of Pittsburgh Press. Poems from *The Apple That Astonished Paris,* by Billy
Collins, are reprinted by permission of the University of Arkansas
Press. Copyright 1988 by Billy Collins.

Grateful acknowledgments are due to the editors of the following
publications where some of these poems first appeared.

The Atlantic Monthly, "The Iron Bridge," "Man Listening to Disc," "Snow
Day"; *Crab Orchard Review,* "Serenade"; *Field,* "Idiomatic," "Scotland";
Five Points, "Pavilion"; *The Gettysburg Review,* "Insomnia," "The Three
Wishes"; *The Paris Review,* "The Butterfly Effect"; *Pif,* "The Flight of the
Reader"; *Ploughshares,* "The Only Day in Existence," "Tomes"; *Poetry,*
"Dharma," "Jealousy," "Madmen," "November," "Reading an Anthology
of Chinese Poems of the Sung Dynasty, I Pause to Admire the Length
and Clarity of Their Titles," "Sonnet"; *The Southern Review,* "The
Waitress"; *The Times Literary Supplement,* "Ignorance"

Library of Congress Cataloging-in-Publication Data
Collins, Billy.
Sailing alone around the room: new and selected poems / Billy Collins.
p.   cm.
ISBN 0-375-75519-5
I. Title.
PS3553.O47478   S25   2000
811'.54—DC21   99-052861

BOOK DESIGN BY BARBARA M. BACHMAN

IN MEMORIAM

Katherine Collins (1901–1997)

William S. Collins (1901–1994)

Contents

FROM *The Apple That Astonished Paris* (1988)

ANOTHER REASON WHY I DON'T KEEP A GUN IN THE HOUSE	3
WALKING ACROSS THE ATLANTIC	4
PLIGHT OF THE TROUBADOUR	5
THE LESSON	6
WINTER SYNTAX	7
ADVICE TO WRITERS	8
THE RIVAL POET	9
INSOMNIA	10
EARTHLING	11
BOOKS	12
BAR TIME	14
MY NUMBER	15
INTRODUCTION TO POETRY	16
THE BROOKLYN MUSEUM OF ART	17
SCHOOLSVILLE	18

FROM *Questions About Angels* (1991)

AMERICAN SONNET	23
QUESTIONS ABOUT ANGELS	24
A HISTORY OF WEATHER	26
THE DEATH OF ALLEGORY	27
FORGETFULNESS	29
CANDLE HAT	30

Student of Clouds   32

The Dead   33

The Man in the Moon   34

The Wires of the Night   35

Vade Mecum   36

Not Touching   37

The History Teacher   38

First Reader   39

Purity   40

Nostalgia   42

FROM *The Art of Drowning* (1995)

Consolation   47

Osso Buco   49

Directions   51

Sunday Morning with the
Sensational Nightingales   53

The Best Cigarette   55

Days   57

Tuesday, June 4, 1991   58

Canada   61

On Turning Ten   63

Workshop   65

My Heart   68

Budapest   69

Dancing Toward Bethlehem   70

Monday Morning   71

Center   72

Design   73

Pinup   74

Piano Lessons   76

The Blues   78

Man in Space   79

NIGHTCLUB   80

SOME FINAL WORDS   82

FROM *Picnic, Lightning* (1998)

FISHING ON THE SUSQUEHANNA IN JULY   87

TO A STRANGER BORN IN SOME
    DISTANT COUNTRY HUNDREDS OF
    YEARS FROM NOW   89

I CHOP SOME PARSLEY WHILE LISTENING
    TO ART BLAKEY'S VERSION OF
    "THREE BLIND MICE"   90

AFTERNOON WITH IRISH COWS   92

MARGINALIA   94

SOME DAYS   97

PICNIC, LIGHTNING   98

MORNING   100

BONSAI   101

SHOVELING SNOW WITH BUDDHA   103

SNOW   105

JAPAN   107

VICTORIA'S SECRET   109

LINES COMPOSED OVER THREE THOUSAND
    MILES FROM TINTERN ABBEY   113

PARADELLE FOR SUSAN   116

LINES LOST AMONG TREES   117

TAKING OFF EMILY DICKINSON'S CLOTHES   119

THE NIGHT HOUSE   121

SPLITTING WOOD   123

THE DEATH OF THE HAT   126

PASSENGERS   128

WHERE I LIVE   130

ARISTOTLE   132

New Poems

DHARMA 137

READING AN ANTHOLOGY OF CHINESE
POEMS OF THE SUNG DYNASTY, I PAUSE
TO ADMIRE THE LENGTH AND CLARITY
OF THEIR TITLES 138

SNOW DAY 140

INSOMNIA 142

MADMEN 144

SONNET 146

IDIOMATIC 147

THE WAITRESS 148

THE BUTTERFLY EFFECT 151

SERENADE 152

THE THREE WISHES 154

PAVILION 156

THE MOVIES 158

JEALOUSY 160

TOMES 162

MAN LISTENING TO DISC 164

SCOTLAND 166

NOVEMBER 168

THE IRON BRIDGE 169

THE FLIGHT OF THE READER 171

FROM

The Apple That Astonished Paris

(1 9 8 8)

Another Reason Why I Don't
Keep a Gun in the House

The neighbors' dog will not stop barking.
He is barking the same high, rhythmic bark
that he barks every time they leave the house.
They must switch him on on their way out.

The neighbors' dog will not stop barking.
I close all the windows in the house
and put on a Beethoven symphony full blast
but I can still hear him muffled under the music,
barking, barking, barking,

and now I can see him sitting in the orchestra,
his head raised confidently as if Beethoven
had included a part for barking dog.

When the record finally ends he is still barking,
sitting there in the oboe section barking,
his eyes fixed on the conductor who is
entreating him with his baton

while the other musicians listen in respectful
silence to the famous barking dog solo,
that endless coda that first established
Beethoven as an innovative genius.

Walking Across
the Atlantic

I wait for the holiday crowd to clear the beach
before stepping onto the first wave.

Soon I am walking across the Atlantic
thinking about Spain,
checking for whales, waterspouts.

I feel the water holding up my shifting weight.
Tonight I will sleep on its rocking surface.

But for now I try to imagine what
this must look like to the fish below,
the bottoms of my feet appearing, disappearing.

Plight of the Troubadour

For a good hour I have been singing lays
in langue d'oc to a woman who knows
only langue d'oïl, an odd Picard dialect
at that.

The European love lyric is flourishing
with every tremor of my voice,
yet a friend has had to tap my shoulder
to tell me she has not caught a word.

My sentiments are tangled like kites
in the branches of her incomprehension,
and soon I will be lost in an anthology
and poets will no longer wear hats like mine.

Provence will be nothing more
than a pink hue on a map or an answer on a test.
And still the woman smiles over at me
feigning this look of sisterly understanding.

The Lesson

In the morning when I found History
snoring heavily on the couch,
I took down his overcoat from the rack
and placed its weight over my shoulder blades.

It would protect me on the cold walk
into the village for milk and the paper
and I figured he would not mind,
not after our long conversation the night before.

How unexpected his blustering anger
when I returned covered with icicles,
the way he rummaged through the huge pockets
making sure no major battle or English queen
had fallen out and become lost in the deep snow.

Winter Syntax

A sentence starts out like a lone traveler
heading into a blizzard at midnight,
tilting into the wind, one arm shielding his face,
the tails of his thin coat flapping behind him.

There are easier ways of making sense,
the connoisseurship of gesture, for example.
You hold a girl's face in your hands like a vase.
You lift a gun from the glove compartment
and toss it out the window into the desert heat.
These cool moments are blazing with silence.

The full moon makes sense. When a cloud crosses it
it becomes as eloquent as a bicycle leaning
outside a drugstore or a dog who sleeps all afternoon
in a corner of the couch.

Bare branches in winter are a form of writing.
The unclothed body is autobiography.
Every lake is a vowel, every island a noun.

But the traveler persists in his misery,
struggling all night through the deepening snow,
leaving a faint alphabet of bootprints
on the white hills and the white floors of valleys,
a message for field mice and passing crows.

At dawn he will spot the vine of smoke
rising from your chimney, and when he stands
before you shivering, draped in sparkling frost,
a smile will appear in the beard of icicles,
and the man will express a complete thought.

Advice to Writers

Even if it keeps you up all night,
wash down the walls and scrub the floor
of your study before composing a syllable.

Clean the place as if the Pope were on his way.
Spotlessness is the niece of inspiration.

The more you clean, the more brilliant
your writing will be, so do not hesitate to take
to the open fields to scour the undersides
of rocks or swab in the dark forest
upper branches, nests full of eggs.

When you find your way back home
and stow the sponges and brushes under the sink,
you will behold in the light of dawn
the immaculate altar of your desk,
a clean surface in the middle of a clean world.

From a small vase, sparkling blue, lift
a yellow pencil, the sharpest of the bouquet,
and cover pages with tiny sentences
like long rows of devoted ants
that followed you in from the woods.

The Rival Poet

The column of your book titles,
always introducing your latest one,
looms over me like Roman architecture.

It is longer than the name
of an Italian countess, longer
than this poem will probably be.

Etched on the head of a pin,
my own production would leave room for
The Lord's Prayer and many dancing angels.
No matter.

In my revenge daydream I am the one
poised on the marble staircase
high above the crowded ballroom.
A retainer in livery announces me
and the Contessa Maria Teresa Isabella
Veronica Multalire Eleganza de Bella Ferrari.

You are the one below
fidgeting in your rented tux
with some local Cindy hanging all over you.

Insomnia

After counting all the sheep in the world
I enumerate the wildebeests, snails,
camels, skylarks, etc.,

then I add up all the zoos and aquariums,
country by country.

By early light I am asleep
in a nightmare about drowning in the Flood,
yelling across the rising water
at preoccupied Noah as his wondrous
ark sails by and begins to grow smaller.

Now a silhouette on the horizon,
the only boat on earth is disappearing.

As I rise and fall on the rocking waves,
I concentrate on the giraffe couple,
their necks craning over the roof,
to keep my life from flashing before me.

After all the animals wink out of sight
I float on my back, eyes closed.
I picture all the fish in creation
leaping a fence in a field of water,
one colorful species after another.

Earthling

You have probably come across
those scales in planetariums
that tell you how much you
would weigh on other planets.

You have noticed the fat ones
lingering on the Mars scale
and the emaciated slowing up
the line for Neptune.

As a creature of average weight,
I fail to see the attraction.

Imagine squatting in the wasteland
of Pluto, all five tons of you,
or wandering around Mercury
wondering what to do next with your ounce.

How much better to step onto
the simple bathroom scale,
a happy earthling feeling
the familiar ropes of gravity,

157 pounds standing soaking wet
a respectful distance from the sun.

Books

From the heart of this dark, evacuated campus
I can hear the library humming in the night,
a choir of authors murmuring inside their books
along the unlit, alphabetical shelves,
Giovanni Pontano next to Pope, Dumas next to his son,
each one stitched into his own private coat,
together forming a low, gigantic chord of language.

I picture a figure in the act of reading,
shoes on a desk, head tilted into the wind of a book,
a man in two worlds, holding the rope of his tie
as the suicide of lovers saturates a page,
or lighting a cigarette in the middle of a theorem.
He moves from paragraph to paragraph
as if touring a house of endless, paneled rooms.

I hear the voice of my mother reading to me
from a chair facing the bed, books about horses and dogs,
and inside her voice lie other distant sounds,
the horrors of a stable ablaze in the night,
a bark that is moving toward the brink of speech.

I watch myself building bookshelves in college,
walls within walls, as rain soaks New England,
or standing in a bookstore in a trench coat.

I see all of us reading ourselves away from ourselves,
straining in circles of light to find more light
until the line of words becomes a trail of crumbs
that we follow across a page of fresh snow;

when evening is shadowing the forest
and small birds flutter down to consume the crumbs,
we have to listen hard to hear the voices
of the boy and his sister receding into the woods.

Bar Time

In keeping with universal saloon practice,
the clock here is set fifteen minutes ahead
of all the clocks in the outside world.

This makes us a rather advanced group,
doing our drinking in the unknown future,
immune from the cares of the present,
safely harbored a quarter of an hour
beyond the woes of the contemporary scene.

No wonder such thoughtless pleasure derives
from tending the small fire of a cigarette,
from observing this glass of whiskey and ice,
the cold rust I am sipping,

or from having an eye on the street outside
when Ordinary Time slouches past in a topcoat,
rain running off the brim of his hat,
the late edition like a flag in his pocket.

My Number

Is Death miles away from this house,
reaching for a widow in Cincinnati
or breathing down the neck of a lost hiker
in British Columbia?

Is he too busy making arrangements,
tampering with air brakes,
scattering cancer cells like seeds,
loosening the wooden beams of roller coasters

to bother with my hidden cottage
that visitors find so hard to find?

Or is he stepping from a black car
parked at the dark end of the lane,
shaking open the familiar cloak,
its hood raised like the head of a crow,
and removing the scythe from the trunk?

Did you have any trouble with the directions?
I will ask, as I start talking my way out of this.

Introduction to Poetry

I ask them to take a poem
and hold it up to the light
like a color slide

or press an ear against its hive.

I say drop a mouse into a poem
and watch him probe his way out,

or walk inside the poem's room
and feel the walls for a light switch.

I want them to water-ski
across the surface of a poem
waving at the author's name on the shore.

But all they want to do
is tie the poem to a chair with rope
and torture a confession out of it.

They begin beating it with a hose
to find out what it really means.

The Brooklyn Museum of Art

I will now step over the soft velvet rope
and walk directly into this massive Hudson River
painting and pick my way along the Palisades
with this stick I snapped off a dead tree.

I will skirt the smoky, nestled towns
and seek the path that leads always outward
until I become lost, without a hope
of ever finding the way back to the museum.

I will stand on the bluffs in nineteenth-century clothes,
a dwarf among rock, hills, and flowing water,
and I will fish from the banks in a straw hat
which will feel like a brush stroke on my head.

And I will hide in the green covers of forests
so no appreciator of Frederick Edwin Church,
leaning over the soft velvet rope,
will spot my tiny figure moving in the stillness
and cry out, pointing for the others to see,

and be thought mad and led away to a cell
where there is no vaulting landscape to explore,
none of this birdsong that halts me in my tracks,
and no wide curving of this river that draws
my steps toward the misty vanishing point.

Schoolsville

Glancing over my shoulder at the past,
I realize the number of students I have taught
is enough to populate a small town.

I can see it nestled in a paper landscape,
chalk dust flurrying down in winter,
nights dark as a blackboard.

The population ages but never graduates.
On hot afternoons they sweat the final in the park
and when it's cold they shiver around stoves
reading disorganized essays out loud.
A bell rings on the hour and everybody zigzags
into the streets with their books.

I forgot all their last names first and their
first names last in alphabetical order.
But the boy who always had his hand up
is an alderman and owns the haberdashery.
The girl who signed her papers in lipstick
leans against the drugstore, smoking,
brushing her hair like a machine.

Their grades are sewn into their clothes
like references to Hawthorne.
The A's stroll along with other A's.
The D's honk whenever they pass another D.

All the creative-writing students recline
on the courthouse lawn and play the lute.
Wherever they go, they form a big circle.

Needless to say, I am the mayor.
I live in the white colonial at Maple and Main.
I rarely leave the house. The car deflates
in the driveway. Vines twirl around the porch swing.

Once in a while a student knocks on the door
with a term paper fifteen years late
or a question about Yeats or double-spacing.
And sometimes one will appear in a windowpane
to watch me lecturing the wallpaper,
quizzing the chandelier, reprimanding the air.

FROM

Questions
About Angels

(1 9 9 1)

American Sonnet

We do not speak like Petrarch or wear a hat like Spenser
and it is not fourteen lines
like furrows in a small, carefully plowed field

but the picture postcard, a poem on vacation,
that forces us to sing our songs in little rooms
or pour our sentiments into measuring cups.

We write on the back of a waterfall or lake,
adding to the view a caption as conventional
as an Elizabethan woman's heliocentric eyes.

We locate an adjective for the weather.
We announce that we are having a wonderful time.
We express the wish that you were here

and hide the wish that we were where you are,
walking back from the mailbox, your head lowered
as you read and turn the thin message in your hands.

A slice of this place, a length of white beach,
a piazza or carved spires of a cathedral
will pierce the familiar place where you remain,

and you will toss on the table this reversible display:
a few square inches of where we have strayed
and a compression of what we feel.

Questions About Angels

Of all the questions you might want to ask
about angels, the only one you ever hear
is how many can dance on the head of a pin.

No curiosity about how they pass the eternal time
besides circling the Throne chanting in Latin
or delivering a crust of bread to a hermit on earth
or guiding a boy and girl across a rickety wooden bridge.

Do they fly through God's body and come out singing?
Do they swing like children from the hinges
of the spirit world saying their names backwards and
    forwards?
Do they sit alone in little gardens changing colors?

What about their sleeping habits, the fabric of their robes,
their diet of unfiltered divine light?
What goes on inside their luminous heads? Is there a wall
these tall presences can look over and see hell?

If an angel fell off a cloud, would he leave a hole
in a river and would the hole float along endlessly
filled with the silent letters of every angelic word?

If an angel delivered the mail, would he arrive
in a blinding rush of wings or would he just assume
the appearance of the regular mailman and
whistle up the driveway reading the postcards?

No, the medieval theologians control the court.
The only question you ever hear is about
the little dance floor on the head of a pin
where halos are meant to converge and drift invisibly.

It is designed to make us think in millions,
billions, to make us run out of numbers and collapse
into infinity, but perhaps the answer is simply one:
one female angel dancing alone in her stocking feet,
a small jazz combo working in the background.

She sways like a branch in the wind, her beautiful
eyes closed, and the tall thin bassist leans over
to glance at his watch because she has been dancing
forever, and now it is very late, even for musicians.

A History of Weather

It is the kind of spring morning—candid sunlight
elucidating the air, a flower-ruffling breeze—
that makes me want to begin a history of weather,
a ten-volume elegy for the atmospheres of the past,
the envelopes that have moved around the moving globe.

It will open by examining the cirrus clouds
that are now sweeping over this house into the next state,
and every chapter will step backwards in time
to illustrate the rain that fell on battlefields
and the winds that attended beheadings, coronations.

The snow flurries of Victorian London will be surveyed
along with the gales that blew off Renaissance caps.
The tornadoes of the Middle Ages will be explicated
and the long, overcast days of the Dark Ages.
There will be a section on the frozen nights of antiquity
and on the heat that shimmered in the deserts of the Bible.

The study will be hailed as ambitious and definitive,
for it will cover even the climate before the Flood
when showers moistened Eden and will conclude
with the mysteries of the weather before history
when unseen clouds drifted over an unpeopled world,
when not a soul lay in any of earth's meadows gazing up
at the passing of enormous faces and animal shapes,
his jacket bunched into a pillow, an open book on his chest.

The Death of Allegory

I am wondering what became of all those tall abstractions
that used to pose, robed and statuesque, in paintings
and parade about on the pages of the Renaissance
displaying their capital letters like license plates.

Truth cantering on a powerful horse,
Chastity, eyes downcast, fluttering with veils.
Each one was marble come to life, a thought in a coat,
Courtesy bowing with one hand always extended,

Villainy sharpening an instrument behind a wall,
Reason with her crown and Constancy alert behind a helm.
They are all retired now, consigned to a Florida for tropes.
Justice is there standing by an open refrigerator.

Valor lies in bed listening to the rain.
Even Death has nothing to do but mend his cloak and hood,
and all their props are locked away in a warehouse,
hourglasses, globes, blindfolds and shackles.

Even if you called them back, there are no places left
for them to go, no Garden of Mirth or Bower of Bliss.
The Valley of Forgiveness is lined with condominiums
and chain saws are howling in the Forest of Despair.

Here on the table near the window is a vase of peonies
and next to it black binoculars and a money clip,
exactly the kind of thing we now prefer,
objects that sit quietly on a line in lower case,

themselves and nothing more, a wheelbarrow,
an empty mailbox, a razor blade resting in a glass ashtray.
As for the others, the great ideas on horseback
and the long-haired virtues in embroidered gowns,

it looks as though they have traveled down
that road you see on the final page of storybooks,
the one that winds up a green hillside and disappears
into an unseen valley where everyone must be fast asleep.

Forgetfulness

The name of the author is the first to go
followed obediently by the title, the plot,
the heartbreaking conclusion, the entire novel
which suddenly becomes one you have never read, never
    even heard of,

as if, one by one, the memories you used to harbor
decided to retire to the southern hemisphere of the brain,
to a little fishing village where there are no phones.

Long ago you kissed the names of the nine Muses good-bye
and watched the quadratic equation pack its bag,
and even now as you memorize the order of the planets,

something else is slipping away, a state flower perhaps,
the address of an uncle, the capital of Paraguay.

Whatever it is you are struggling to remember
it is not poised on the tip of your tongue,
not even lurking in some obscure corner of your spleen.

It has floated away down a dark mythological river
whose name begins with an *L* as far as you can recall,
well on your own way to oblivion where you will join those
who have even forgotten how to swim and how to ride a
    bicycle.

No wonder you rise in the middle of the night
to look up the date of a famous battle in a book on war.
No wonder the moon in the window seems to have drifted
out of a love poem that you used to know by heart.

Candle Hat

In most self-portraits it is the face that dominates:
Cézanne is a pair of eyes swimming in brushstrokes,
Van Gogh stares out of a halo of swirling darkness,
Rembrandt looks relieved, as if he were taking a breather
from painting *The Blinding of Samson.*

But in this one Goya stands well back from the mirror
and is seen posed in the clutter of his studio
addressing a canvas tilted back on a tall easel.

He appears to be smiling out at us as if he knew
we would be amused by the extraordinary hat on his head
which is fitted around the brim with candle holders,
a device that allowed him to work into the night.

You can only wonder what it would be like
to be wearing such a chandelier on your head
as if you were a walking dining room or concert hall.

But once you see this hat there is no need to read
any biography of Goya or to memorize his dates.

To understand Goya you only have to imagine him
lighting the candles one by one, then placing
the hat on his head, ready for a night of work.

Imagine him surprising his wife with his new invention,
then laughing like a birthday cake when she saw the glow.
Imagine him flickering through the rooms of his house
with all the shadows flying across the walls.

Imagine a lost traveler knocking on his door
one dark night in the hill country of Spain.
"Come in," he would say, "I was just painting myself,"
as he stood in the doorway holding up the wand of a brush,
illuminated in the blaze of his famous candle hat.

Student of Clouds

The emotion is to be found in the clouds,
not in the green solids of the sloping hills
or even in the gray signatures of rivers,
according to Constable, who was a student of clouds
and filled shelves of sketchbooks with their motion,
their lofty gesturing and sudden implication of weather.

Outdoors, he must have looked up thousands of times,
his pencil trying to keep pace with their high voyaging
and the silent commotion of their eddying and flow.
Clouds would move beyond the outlines he would draw
as they moved within themselves, tumbling into their centers
and swirling off at the burning edges in vapors
to dissipate into the universal blue of the sky.

In photographs we can stop all this movement now
long enough to tag them with their Latin names.
Cirrus, nimbus, stratocumulus—
dizzying, romantic, authoritarian—
they bear their titles over the schoolhouses below
where their shapes and meanings are memorized.

High on the soft blue canvases of Constable
they are stuck in pigment, but his clouds appear
to be moving still in the wind of his brush,
inching out of England and the nineteenth century
and sailing over these meadows where I am walking,
bareheaded beneath this cupola of motion,
my thoughts arranged like paint on a high blue ceiling.

The Dead

The dead are always looking down on us, they say,
while we are putting on our shoes or making a sandwich,
they are looking down through the glass-bottom boats
    of heaven
as they row themselves slowly through eternity.

They watch the tops of our heads moving below on earth,
and when we lie down in a field or on a couch,
drugged perhaps by the hum of a warm afternoon,
they think we are looking back at them,

which makes them lift their oars and fall silent
and wait, like parents, for us to close our eyes.

The Man in the Moon

He used to frighten me in the nights of childhood,
the wide adult face, enormous, stern, aloft.
I could not imagine such loneliness, such coldness.

But tonight as I drive home over these hilly roads
I see him sinking behind stands of winter trees
and rising again to show his familiar face.

And when he comes into full view over open fields
he looks like a young man who has fallen in love
with the dark earth,

a pale bachelor, well-groomed and full of melancholy,
his round mouth open
as if he had just broken into song.

The Wires of the Night

I thought about his death for so many hours,
tangled there in the wires of the night,
that it came to have a body and dimensions,
more than a voice shaking over the telephone
or the black obituary boldface of name and dates.

His death now had an entrance and an exit,
    doors and stairs,
windows and shutters which are the motionless wings
of windows. His death had a head and clothes,
the white shirt and baggy trousers of death.

His death had pages, a dark leather cover, an index,
and the print was too minuscule for anyone to read.
His death had hinges and bolts that were oiled
    and locked,
had a loud motor, four tires, an antenna that listened
to the wind, and a mirror in which you could see the past.

His death had sockets and keys, it had walls and beams.
It had a handle which you could not hold and a floor
you could not lie down on in the middle of the night.

In the freakish pink and gray of dawn I took
his death to bed with me and his death was my bed
and in every corner of the room it hid from the light,

and then it was the light of day and the next day
and all the days to follow, and it moved into the future
like the sharp tip of a pen moving across an empty page.

Vade Mecum

I want the scissors to be sharp
and the table to be perfectly level
when you cut me out of my life
and paste me in that book you always carry.

Not Touching

The valentine of desire is pasted over my heart
and still we are not touching, like things

in a poorly done still life
where the knife appears to be floating over the plate
which is itself hovering above the table somehow,

the entire arrangement of apple, pear, and wineglass
having forgotten the law of gravity,
refusing to be still,

as if the painter had caught them all
in a rare moment of slow flight
just before they drifted out of the room
through a window of perfectly realistic sunlight.

The History Teacher

Trying to protect his students' innocence
he told them the Ice Age was really just
the Chilly Age, a period of a million years
when everyone had to wear sweaters.

And the Stone Age became the Gravel Age,
named after the long driveways of the time.

The Spanish Inquisition was nothing more
than an outbreak of questions such as
"How far is it from here to Madrid?"
"What do you call the matador's hat?"

The War of the Roses took place in a garden,
and the Enola Gay dropped one tiny atom
on Japan.

The children would leave his classroom
for the playground to torment the weak
and the smart,
mussing up their hair and breaking their glasses,

while he gathered up his notes and walked home
past flower beds and white picket fences,
wondering if they would believe that soldiers
in the Boer War told long, rambling stories
designed to make the enemy nod off.

First Reader

I can see them standing politely on the wide pages
that I was still learning to turn,
Jane in a blue jumper, Dick with his crayon-brown hair,
playing with a ball or exploring the cosmos
of the backyard, unaware they are the first characters,
the boy and girl who begin fiction.

Beyond the simple illustration of their neighborhood
the other protagonists were waiting in a huddle:
frightening Heathcliff, frightened Pip, Nick Adams
carrying a fishing rod, Emma Bovary riding into Rouen.

But I would read about the perfect boy and his sister
even before I would read about Adam and Eve, garden
    and gate,
and before I heard the name Gutenberg, the type
of their simple talk was moving into my focusing eyes.

It was always Saturday and he and she
were always pointing at something and shouting "Look!"
pointing at the dog, the bicycle, or at their father
as he pushed a hand mower over the lawn,
waving at aproned Mother framed in the kitchen doorway,
pointing toward the sky, pointing at each other.

They wanted us to look but we had looked already
and seen the shaded lawn, the wagon, the postman.
We had seen the dog, walked, watered, and fed the animal,
and now it was time to discover the infinite, clicking
permutations of the alphabet's small and capital letters.
Alphabetical ourselves in the rows of classroom desks,
we were forgetting how to look, learning how to read.

Purity

My favorite time to write is in the late afternoon,
weekdays, particularly Wednesdays.
This is how I go about it:
I take a fresh pot of tea into my study and close the door.
Then I remove my clothes and leave them in a pile
as if I had melted to death and my legacy consisted of only
a white shirt, a pair of pants, and a pot of cold tea.

Then I remove my flesh and hang it over a chair.
I slide it off my bones like a silken garment.
I do this so that what I write will be pure,
completely rinsed of the carnal,
uncontaminated by the preoccupations of the body.

Finally I remove each of my organs and arrange them
on a small table near the window.
I do not want to hear their ancient rhythms
when I am trying to tap out my own drumbeat.

Now I sit down at the desk, ready to begin.
I am entirely pure: nothing but a skeleton at a typewriter.

I should mention that sometimes I leave my penis on.
I find it difficult to ignore the temptation.
Then I am a skeleton with a penis at a typewriter.

In this condition I write extraordinary love poems,
most of them exploiting the connection between sex
    and death.

I am concentration itself: I exist in a universe
where there is nothing but sex, death, and typewriting.

After a spell of this I remove my penis too.
Then I am all skull and bones typing into the afternoon.
Just the absolute essentials, no flounces.
Now I write only about death, most classical of themes
in language light as the air between my ribs.

Afterward, I reward myself by going for a drive at sunset.
I replace my organs and slip back into my flesh
and clothes. Then I back the car out of the garage
and speed through woods on winding country roads,
passing stone walls, farmhouses, and frozen ponds,
all perfectly arranged like words in a famous sonnet.

Nostalgia

Remember the 1340s? We were doing a dance called
   the Catapult.
You always wore brown, the color craze of the decade,
and I was draped in one of those capes that were popular,
the ones with unicorns and pomegranates in needlework.
Everyone would pause for beer and onions in the afternoon,
and at night we would play a game called "Find the Cow."
Everything was hand-lettered then, not like today.

Where has the summer of 1572 gone? Brocade and sonnet
marathons were the rage. We used to dress up in the flags
of rival baronies and conquer one another in cold rooms
   of stone.
Out on the dance floor we were all doing the Struggle
while your sister practiced the Daphne all alone in her room.
We borrowed the jargon of farriers for our slang.
These days language seems transparent, a badly broken code.

The 1790s will never come again. Childhood was big.
People would take walks to the very tops of hills
and write down what they saw in their journals without
   speaking.
Our collars were high and our hats were extremely soft.
We would surprise each other with alphabets made of twigs.
It was a wonderful time to be alive, or even dead.

I am very fond of the period between 1815 and 1821.
Europe trembled while we sat still for our portraits.
And I would love to return to 1901 if only for a moment,
time enough to wind up a music box and do a
   few dance steps,

or shoot me back to 1922 or 1941, or at least let me
recapture the serenity of last month when we picked
berries and glided through afternoons in a canoe.

Even this morning would be an improvement over
    the present.
I was in the garden then, surrounded by the hum of bees
and the Latin names of flowers, watching the early light
flash off the slanted windows of the greenhouse
and silver the limbs on the rows of dark hemlocks.

As usual, I was thinking about the moments of the past,
letting my memory rush over them like water
rushing over the stones on the bottom of a stream.
I was even thinking a little about the future, that place
where people are doing a dance we cannot imagine,
a dance whose name we can only guess.

The Art of Drowning

(1 9 9 5)

Consolation

How agreeable it is not to be touring Italy this summer,
wandering her cities and ascending her torrid hill towns.
How much better to cruise these local, familiar streets,
fully grasping the meaning of every road sign and billboard
and all the sudden hand gestures of my compatriots.

There are no abbeys here, no crumbling frescoes or famous
domes and there is no need to memorize a succession
of kings or tour the dripping corners of a dungeon.
No need to stand around a sarcophagus, see Napoleon's
little bed on Elba, or view the bones of a saint under glass.

How much better to command the simple precinct of home
than be dwarfed by pillar, arch, and basilica.
Why hide my head in phrase books and wrinkled maps?
Why feed scenery into a hungry, one-eyed camera
eager to eat the world one monument at a time?

Instead of slouching in a café ignorant of the word for ice,
I will head down to the coffee shop and the waitress
known as Dot. I will slide into the flow of the morning
paper, all language barriers down,
rivers of idiom running freely, eggs over easy on the way.

And after breakfast, I will not have to find someone
willing to photograph me with my arm around the owner.
I will not puzzle over the bill or record in a journal
what I had to eat and how the sun came in the window.
It is enough to climb back into the car

as if it were the great car of English itself
and sounding my loud vernacular horn, speed off
down a road that will never lead to Rome, not even Bologna.

Osso Buco

I love the sound of the bone against the plate
and the fortress-like look of it
lying before me in a moat of risotto,
the meat soft as the leg of an angel
who has lived a purely airborne existence.
And best of all, the secret marrow,
the invaded privacy of the animal
prized out with a knife and swallowed down
with cold, exhilarating wine.

I am swaying now in the hour after dinner,
a citizen tilted back on his chair,
a creature with a full stomach—
something you don't hear much about in poetry,
that sanctuary of hunger and deprivation.
You know: the driving rain, the boots by the door,
small birds searching for berries in winter.

But tonight, the lion of contentment
has placed a warm, heavy paw on my chest,
and I can only close my eyes and listen
to the drums of woe throbbing in the distance
and the sound of my wife's laughter
on the telephone in the next room,
the woman who cooked the savory osso buco,
who pointed to show the butcher the ones she wanted.
She who talks to her faraway friend
while I linger here at the table
with a hot, companionable cup of tea,
feeling like one of the friendly natives,
a reliable guide, maybe even the chief's favorite son.

Somewhere, a man is crawling up a rocky hillside
on bleeding knees and palms, an Irish penitent
carrying the stone of the world in his stomach;
and elsewhere people of all nations stare
at one another across a long, empty table.

But here, the candles give off their warm glow,
the same light that Shakespeare and Izaak Walton wrote by,
the light that lit and shadowed the faces of history.
Only now it plays on the blue plates,
the crumpled napkins, the crossed knife and fork.

In a while, one of us will go up to bed
and the other one will follow.
Then we will slip below the surface of the night
into miles of water, drifting down and down
to the dark, soundless bottom
until the weight of dreams pulls us lower still,
below the shale and layered rock,
beneath the strata of hunger and pleasure,
into the broken bones of the earth itself,
into the marrow of the only place we know.

Directions

You know the brick path in back of the house,
the one you see from the kitchen window,
the one that bends around the far end of the garden
where all the yellow primroses are?
And you know how if you leave the path
and walk up into the woods you come
to a heap of rocks, probably pushed
down during the horrors of the Ice Age,
and a grove of tall hemlocks, dark green now
against the light-brown fallen leaves?
And farther on, you know
the small footbridge with the broken railing
and if you go beyond that you arrive
at the bottom of that sheep's head hill?
Well, if you start climbing, and you
might have to grab hold of a sapling
when the going gets steep,
you will eventually come to a long stone
ridge with a border of pine trees
which is as high as you can go
and a good enough place to stop.

The best time is late afternoon
when the sun strobes through
the columns of trees as you are hiking up,
and when you find an agreeable rock
to sit on, you will be able to see
the light pouring down into the woods
and breaking into the shapes and tones
of things and you will hear nothing
but a sprig of birdsong or the leafy

falling of a cone or nut through the trees,
and if this is your day you might even
spot a hare or feel the wing-beats of geese
driving overhead toward some destination.

But it is hard to speak of these things
how the voices of light enter the body
and begin to recite their stories
how the earth holds us painfully against
its breast made of humus and brambles
how we who will soon be gone regard
the entities that continue to return
greener than ever, spring water flowing
through a meadow and the shadows of clouds
passing over the hills and the ground
where we stand in the tremble of thought
taking the vast outside into ourselves.

Still, let me know before you set out.
Come knock on my door
and I will walk with you as far as the garden
with one hand on your shoulder.
I will even watch after you and not turn back
to the house until you disappear
into the crowd of maple and ash,
heading up toward the hill,
piercing the ground with your stick.

Sunday Morning with the
Sensational Nightingales

It was not the Five Mississippi Blind Boys
who lifted me off the ground
that Sunday morning
as I drove down for the paper, some oranges, and bread.
Nor was it the Dixie Hummingbirds
or the Soul Stirrers, despite their quickening name,
or even the Swan Silvertones
who inspired me to look over the commotion of trees
into the open vault of the sky.

No, it was the Sensational Nightingales
who happened to be singing on the gospel
station early that Sunday morning
and must be credited with the bumping up
of my spirit, the arousal of the mice within.

I have always loved this harmony,
like four, sometimes five trains running
side by side over a contoured landscape—
make that a shimmering, red-dirt landscape,
wildflowers growing along the silver tracks,
lace tablecloths covering the hills,
the men and women in white shirts and dresses
walking in the direction of a tall steeple.
Sunday morning in a perfect Georgia.

But I am not here to describe the sound
of the falsetto whine, sepulchral bass,
alto and tenor fitted snugly in between;

only to witness my own minor ascension
that morning as they sang, so parallel,
about the usual themes,
the garden of suffering,
the beads of blood on the forehead,
the stone before the hillside tomb,
and the ancient rolling waters
we would all have to cross some day.

God bless the Sensational Nightingales,
I thought as I turned up the volume,
God bless their families and their powder blue suits.
They are a far cry from the quiet kneeling
I was raised with,
a far, hand-clapping cry from the candles
that glowed in the alcoves
and the fixed eyes of saints staring down
from their corners.

Oh, my cap was on straight that Sunday morning
and I was fine keeping the car on the road.
No one would ever have guessed
I was being lifted into the air by nightingales,
hoisted by their beaks like a long banner
that curls across an empty blue sky,
caught up in the annunciation
of these high, most encouraging tidings.

The Best Cigarette

There are many that I miss,
having sent my last one out a car window
sparking along the road one night, years ago.

The heralded ones, of course:
after sex, the two glowing tips
now the lights of a single ship;
at the end of a long dinner
with more wine to come
and a smoke ring coasting into the chandelier;
or on a white beach,
holding one with fingers still wet from a swim.

How bittersweet these punctuations
of flame and gesture;
but the best were on those mornings
when I would have a little something going
in the typewriter,
the sun bright in the windows,
maybe some Berlioz on in the background.
I would go into the kitchen for coffee
and on the way back to the page,
curled in its roller,
I would light one up and feel
its dry rush mix with the dark taste of coffee.

Then I would be my own locomotive,
trailing behind me as I returned to work
little puffs of smoke,
indicators of progress,
signs of industry and thought,

the signal that told the nineteenth century
it was moving forward.
That was the best cigarette,
when I would steam into the study
full of vaporous hope
and stand there,
the big headlamp of my face
pointed down at all the words in parallel lines.

Days

Each one *is* a gift, no doubt,
mysteriously placed in your waking hand
or set upon your forehead
moments before you open your eyes.

Today begins cold and bright,
the ground heavy with snow
and the thick masonry of ice,
the sun glinting off the turrets of clouds.

Through the calm eye of the window
everything is in its place
but so precariously
this day might be resting somehow

on the one before it,
all the days of the past stacked high
like the impossible tower of dishes
entertainers used to build on stage.

No wonder you find yourself
perched on the top of a tall ladder
hoping to add one more.
Just another Wednesday,

you whisper,
then holding your breath,
place this cup on yesterday's saucer
without the slightest clink.

Tuesday, June 4, 1991

By the time I get myself out of bed, my wife has left
the house to take her botany final and the painter
has arrived in his van and is already painting
the columns of the front porch white and the decking gray.

It is early June, a breezy and sun-riddled Tuesday
that would quickly be forgotten were it not for my
writing these few things down as I sit here empty-headed
at the typewriter with a cup of coffee, light and sweet.

I feel like the secretary to the morning whose only
responsibility is to take down its bright, airy dictation
until it's time to go to lunch with the other girls,
all of us ordering the cottage cheese with half a pear.

This is what stenographers do in courtrooms, too,
alert at their miniature machines taking down every word.
When there is a silence they sit still as I do, waiting
and listening, fingers resting lightly on the keys.

This is also what Samuel Pepys did, jotting down in
private ciphers minor events that would have otherwise
slipped into the dark amnesiac waters of the Thames.
His vigilance finally paid off when London caught fire

as mine does when the painter comes in for coffee
and says how much he likes this slow vocal rendition
of "You Don't Know What Love Is" and I figure I will
make him a tape when he goes back to his brushes and pails.

Under the music I can hear the rush of cars and trucks
on the highway and every so often the new kitten, Felix,
hops into my lap and watches my fingers drumming out
a running record of this particular June Tuesday

as it unrolls before my eyes, a long intricate carpet
that I am walking on slowly with my head bowed
knowing that it is leading me to the quiet shrine
of the afternoon and the melancholy candles of evening.

If I look up, I see out the window the white stars
of clematis climbing a ladder of strings, a woodpile,
a stack of faded bricks, a small green garden of herbs,
things you would expect to find outside a window,

all written down now and placed in the setting
of a stanza as unalterably as they are seated
in their chairs in the ontological rooms of the world.
Yes, this is the kind of job I could succeed in,

an unpaid but contented amanuensis whose hands
are two birds fluttering on the lettered keys,
whose eyes see sunlight splashing through the leaves,
and the bright pink asterisks of honeysuckle

and the piano at the other end of this room with
its small vase of faded flowers and its empty bench.
So convinced am I that I have found my vocation,
tomorrow I will begin my chronicling earlier, at dawn,

a time when hangmen and farmers are up and doing,
when men holding pistols stand in a field back to back.
It is the time the ancients imagined in robes, as Eos
or Aurora, who would leave her sleeping husband in bed,

not to take her botany final, but to pull the sun,
her brother, over the horizon's brilliant rim,
her four-horse chariot aimed at the zenith of the sky.
But tomorrow, dawn will come the way I picture her,

barefoot and disheveled, standing outside my window
in one of the fragile cotton dresses of the poor.
She will look in at me with her thin arms extended,
offering a handful of birdsong and a small cup of light.

Canada

I am writing this on a strip of white birch bark
that I cut from a tree with a penknife.
There is no other way to express adequately
the immensity of the clouds that are passing over the farms
and wooded lakes of Ontario and the endless visibility
that hands you the horizon on a platter.

I am also writing this in a wooden canoe,
a point of balance in the middle of Lake Couchiching,
resting the birch bark against my knees.
I can feel the sun's hands on my bare back,
but I am thinking of winter,
snow piled up in all the provinces
and the solemnity of the long grain-ships
that pass the cold months moored at Owen Sound.

O Canada, as the anthem goes,
scene of my boyhood summers,
you are the pack of Sweet Caporals on the table,
you are the dove-soft train whistle in the night,
you are the empty chair at the end of an empty dock.
You are the shelves of books in a lakeside cottage:
Gift from the Sea by Anne Morrow Lindbergh,
A Child's Garden of Verses by Robert Louis Stevenson,
Ann of Avonlea by L. M. Montgomery,
So You're Going to Paris! by Clara E. Laughlin,
and *Peril Over the Airport,* one
of the Vicky Barr Flight Stewardess series
by Helen Wills whom some will remember
as the author of the Cherry Ames Nurse stories.

What has become of the languorous girls
who would pass the long limp summer evenings reading
Cherry Ames, Student Nurse, Cherry Ames, Senior Nurse,
Cherry Ames, Chief Nurse, and *Cherry Ames, Flight Nurse?*
Where are they now, the ones who shared her adventures
as a veterans' nurse, private duty nurse, visiting nurse,
cruise nurse, night supervisor, mountaineer nurse,
dude ranch nurse (there is little she has not done),
rest home nurse, department store nurse,
boarding school nurse, and country doctor's nurse?

O Canada, I have not forgotten you,
and as I kneel in my canoe, beholding this vision
of a bookcase, I pray that I remain in your vast,
polar, North American memory.
You are the paddle, the snowshoe, the cabin in the pines.
You are Jean de Brébeuf with his martyr's necklace of
      hatchet heads.
You are the moose in the clearing and the moosehead on
      the wall.
You are the rapids, the propeller, the kerosene lamp.
You are the dust that coats the roadside berries.
But not only that.
You are the two boys with pails walking along that road,
and one of them, the taller one minus the straw hat, is me.

On Turning Ten

The whole idea of it makes me feel
like I'm coming down with something,
something worse than any stomach ache
or the headaches I get from reading in bad light—
a kind of measles of the spirit,
a mumps of the psyche,
a disfiguring chicken pox of the soul.

You tell me it is too early to be looking back,
but that is because you have forgotten
the perfect simplicity of being one
and the beautiful complexity introduced by two.
But I can lie on my bed and remember every digit.
At four I was an Arabian wizard.
I could make myself invisible
by drinking a glass of milk a certain way.
At seven I was a soldier, at nine a prince.

But now I am mostly at the window
watching the late afternoon light.
Back then it never fell so solemnly
against the side of my tree house,
and my bicycle never leaned against the garage
as it does today,
all the dark blue speed drained out of it.

This is the beginning of sadness, I say to myself,
as I walk through the universe in my sneakers.
It is time to say good-bye to my imaginary friends,
time to turn the first big number.

It seems only yesterday I used to believe
there was nothing under my skin but light.
If you cut me I would shine.
But now when I fall upon the sidewalks of life,
I skin my knees. I bleed.

Workshop

I might as well begin by saying how much I like the title.
It gets me right away because I'm in a workshop now
so immediately the poem has my attention,
like the Ancient Mariner grabbing me by the sleeve.

And I like the first couple of stanzas,
the way they establish this mode of self-pointing
that runs through the whole poem
and tells us that words are food thrown down
on the ground for other words to eat.
I can almost taste the tail of the snake
in its own mouth,
if you know what I mean.

But what I'm not sure about is the voice,
which sounds in places very casual, very blue jeans,
but other times seems standoffish,
professorial in the worst sense of the word
like the poem is blowing pipe smoke in my face.
But maybe that's just what it wants to do.

What I did find engaging were the middle stanzas,
especially the fourth one.
I like the image of clouds flying like lozenges
which gives me a very clear picture.
And I really like how this drawbridge operator
just appears out of the blue
with his feet up on the iron railing
and his fishing pole jigging—I like jigging—
a hook in the slow industrial canal below.
I love slow industrial canal below. All those *l*'s.

Maybe it's just me,
but the next stanza is where I start to have a problem.
I mean how can the evening bump into the stars?
And what's an obbligato of snow?
Also, I roam the decaffeinated streets.
At that point I'm lost. I need help.

The other thing that throws me off,
and maybe this is just me,
is the way the scene keeps shifting around.
First, we're in this big aerodrome
and the speaker is inspecting a row of dirigibles,
which makes me think this could be a dream.
Then he takes us into his garden,
the part with the dahlias and the coiling hose,
though that's nice, the coiling hose,
but then I'm not sure where we're supposed to be.
The rain and the mint green light,
that makes it feel outdoors, but what about this wallpaper?
Or is it a kind of indoor cemetery?
There's something about death going on here.

In fact, I start to wonder if what we have here
is really two poems, or three, or four,
or possibly none.

But then there's that last stanza, my favorite.
This is where the poem wins me back,
especially the lines spoken in the voice of the mouse.
I mean we've all seen these images in cartoons before,

but I still love the details he uses
when he's describing where he lives.
The perfect little arch of an entrance in the baseboard,
the bed made out of a curled-back sardine can,
the spool of thread for a table.
I start thinking about how hard the mouse had to work
night after night collecting all these things
while the people in the house were fast asleep,
and that gives me a very strong feeling,
a very powerful sense of something.
But I don't know if anyone else was feeling that.
Maybe that was just me.
Maybe that's just the way I read it.

My Heart

It has a bronze covering inlaid with silver,
originally gilt;
the sides are decorated with openwork zoomorphic
panels depicting events in the history
of an unknown religion.
The convoluted top-piece shows a high
level of relief articulation
as do the interworked spirals at the edges.

It was presumably carried in the house-shaped
reliquary alongside it, an object of exceptional
ornament, one of the few such pieces extant.
The handle, worn smooth, indicates its use
in long-forgotten rituals, perhaps
of a sacrificial nature.

It is engirdled with an inventive example
of gold interlacing, no doubt of Celtic influence.
Previously thought to be a pre-Carolingian work,
it is now considered to be of more recent provenance,
probably the early 1940s.

The ball at the center, visible
through the interstices of the lead webbing
and the elaborate copper grillwork,
is composed possibly of jelly
or an early version of water,
certainly a liquid, remarkably suspended
within the intricate craftsmanship of its encasement.

Budapest

My pen moves along the page
like the snout of a strange animal
shaped like a human arm
and dressed in the sleeve of a loose green sweater.

I watch it sniffing the paper ceaselessly,
intent as any forager that has nothing
on its mind but the grubs and insects
that will allow it to live another day.

It wants only to be here tomorrow,
dressed perhaps in the sleeve of a plaid shirt,
nose pressed against the page,
writing a few more dutiful lines

while I gaze out the window and imagine Budapest
or some other city where I have never been.

Dancing Toward Bethlehem

If there is only enough time in the final
minutes of the twentieth century for one last dance
I would like to be dancing it slowly with you,

say, in the ballroom of a seaside hotel.
My palm would press into the small of your back
as the past hundred years collapsed into a pile
of mirrors or buttons or frivolous shoes,

just as the floor of the nineteenth century gave way
and disappeared in a red cloud of brick dust.
There will be no time to order another drink
or worry about what was never said,

not with the orchestra sliding into the sea
and all our attention devoted to humming
whatever it was they were playing.

Monday Morning

The complacency of this student, late
for the final, who chews her pen for an hour,
who sits in her sunny chair,
with a container of coffee and an orange,
a cockatoo swinging freely in her green mind
as if on some drug dissolved,
mingling to give her a wholly ancient rush.
She dreams a little and she fears the mark
she might well get—a catastrophe—
as a frown darkens the hauteur of her light brow.
The orange peels and her bright senior ring
make her think of some procession of classmates,
walking across the wide campus, without a sound,
stalled for the passing of her sneakered feet
over the lawn, to silent pals and steins,
dorm of nobody who would bother to pull an A or care.

Center

At the first chink of sunrise,
the windows on one side of the house
are frosted with stark orange light,

and in every pale blue window
on the other side
a full moon hangs, a round, white blaze.

I look out one side, then the other,
moving from room to room
as if between countries or parts of my life.

Then I stop and stand in the middle,
extend both arms
like Leonardo's man, naked in a perfect circle.

And when I begin to turn slowly
I can feel the whole house turning with me,
rotating free of the earth.

The sun and moon in all the windows
move, too, with the tips of my fingers,
the solar system turning by degrees

with me, morning's egomaniac,
turning on the hallway carpet in my slippers,
taking the cold orange, blue, and white

for a quiet, unhurried spin,
all wheel and compass, axis and reel,
as wide awake as I will ever be.

Design

I pour a coating of salt on the table
and make a circle in it with my finger.
This is the cycle of life
I say to no one.
This is the wheel of fortune,
the Arctic Circle.
This is the ring of Kerry
and the white rose of Tralee
I say to the ghosts of my family,
the dead fathers,
the aunt who drowned,
my unborn brothers and sisters,
my unborn children.
This is the sun with its glittering spokes
and the bitter moon.
This is the absolute circle of geometry
I say to the crack in the wall,
to the birds who cross the window.
This is the wheel I just invented
to roll through the rest of my life
I say
touching my finger to my tongue.

Pinup

The murkiness of the local garage is not so dense
that you cannot make out the calendar of pinup
drawings on the wall above a bench of tools.
Your ears are ringing with the sound of
the mechanic hammering on your exhaust pipe,
and as you look closer you notice that this month's
is not the one pushing the lawn mower, wearing
a straw hat and very short blue shorts,
her shirt tied in a knot just below her breasts.
Nor is it the one in the admiral's cap, bending
forward, resting her hands on a wharf piling,
glancing over the tiny anchors on her shoulders.
No, this is March, the month of great winds,
so appropriately it is the one walking her dog
along a city sidewalk on a very blustery day.
One hand is busy keeping her hat down on her head
and the other is grasping the little dog's leash,
so of course there is no hand left to push down
her dress which is billowing up around her waist
exposing her long stockinged legs and yes the secret
apparatus of her garter belt. Needless to say,
in the confusion of wind and excited dog
the leash has wrapped itself around her ankles
several times giving her a rather bridled
and helpless appearance which is added to
by the impossibly high heels she is teetering on.
You would like to come to her rescue,
gather up the little dog in your arms,
untangle the leash, lead her to safety,
and receive her bottomless gratitude, but
the mechanic is calling you over to look

at something under your car. It seems that he has
run into a problem and the job is going
to cost more than he had said and take
much longer than he had thought.
Well, it can't be helped, you hear yourself say
as you return to your place by the workbench,
knowing that as soon as the hammering resumes
you will slowly lift the bottom of the calendar
just enough to reveal a glimpse of what
the future holds in store: ah,
the red polka-dot umbrella of April and her
upturned palm extended coyly into the rain.

Piano Lessons

1

My teacher lies on the floor with a bad back
off to the side of the piano.
I sit up straight on the stool.
He begins by telling me that every key
is like a different room
and I am a blind man who must learn
to walk through all twelve of them
without hitting the furniture.
I feel myself reach for the first doorknob.

2

He tells me that every scale has a shape
and I have to learn how to hold
each one in my hands.
At home I practice with my eyes closed.
C is an open book.
D is a vase with two handles.
G flat is a black boot.
E has the legs of a bird.

3

He says the scale is the mother of the chords.
I can see her pacing the bedroom floor
waiting for her children to come home.
They are out at nightclubs shading and lighting
all the songs while couples dance slowly
or stare at one another across tables.
This is the way it must be. After all,
just the right chord can bring you to tears
but no one listens to the scales,
no one listens to their mother.

4

I am doing my scales,
the familiar anthems of childhood.
My fingers climb the ladder of notes
and come back down without turning around.
Anyone walking under this open window
would picture a girl of about ten
sitting at the keyboard with perfect posture,
not me slumped over in my bathrobe, disheveled,
like a white Horace Silver.

5

I am learning to play
"It Might As Well Be Spring"
but my left hand would rather be jingling
the change in the darkness of my pocket
or taking a nap on an armrest.
I have to drag him into the music
like a difficult and neglected child.
This is the revenge of the one who never gets
to hold the pen or wave good-bye,
and now, who never gets to play the melody.

6

Even when I am not playing, I think about the piano.
It is the largest, heaviest,
and most beautiful object in this house.
I pause in the doorway just to take it all in.
And late at night I picture it downstairs,
this hallucination standing on three legs,
this curious beast with its enormous moonlit smile.

The Blues

Much of what is said here
must be said twice,
a reminder that no one
takes an immediate interest in the pain of others.

Nobody will listen, it would seem,
if you simply admit
your baby left you early this morning
she didn't even stop to say good-bye.

But if you sing it again
with the help of the band
which will now lift you to a higher,
more ardent and beseeching key,

people will not only listen;
they will shift to the sympathetic
edges of their chairs,
moved to such acute anticipation

by that chord and the delay that follows,
they will not be able to sleep
unless you release with one finger
a scream from the throat of your guitar

and turn your head back to the microphone
to let them know
you're a hard-hearted man
but that woman's sure going to make you cry.

Man in Space

All you have to do is listen to the way a man
sometimes talks to his wife at a table of people
and notice how intent he is on making his point
even though her lower lip is beginning to quiver,

and you will know why the women in science
fiction movies who inhabit a planet of their own
are not pictured making a salad or reading a magazine
when the men from earth arrive in their rocket,

why they are always standing in a semicircle
with their arms folded, their bare legs set apart,
their breasts protected by hard metal disks.

Nightclub

You are so beautiful and I am a fool
to be in love with you
is a theme that keeps coming up
in songs and poems.
There seems to be no room for variation.
I have never heard anyone sing
I am so beautiful
and you are a fool to be in love with me,
even though this notion has surely
crossed the minds of women and men alike.
You are so beautiful, too bad you are a fool
is another one you don't hear.
Or, you are a fool to consider me beautiful.
That one you will never hear, guaranteed.

For no particular reason this afternoon
I am listening to Johnny Hartman
whose dark voice can curl around
the concepts of love, beauty, and foolishness
like no one else's can.
It feels like smoke curling up from a cigarette
someone left burning on a baby grand piano
around three o'clock in the morning;
smoke that billows up into the bright lights
while out there in the darkness
some of the beautiful fools have gathered
around little tables to listen,
some with their eyes closed,
others leaning forward into the music
as if it were holding them up,
or twirling the loose ice in a glass,

slipping by degrees into a rhythmic dream.
Yes, there is all this foolish beauty,
borne beyond midnight,
that has no desire to go home,
especially now when everyone in the room
is watching the large man with the tenor sax
that hangs from his neck like a golden fish.
He moves forward to the edge of the stage
and hands the instrument down to me
and nods that I should play.
So I put the mouthpiece to my lips
and blow into it with all my living breath.
We are all so foolish,
my long bebop solo begins by saying,
so damn foolish
we have become beautiful without even knowing it.

Some Final Words

I cannot leave you without saying this:
the past is nothing,
a nonmemory, a phantom,
a soundproof closet in which Johann Strauss
is composing another waltz no one can hear.

It is a fabrication, best forgotten,
a wellspring of sorrow
that waters a field of bitter vegetation.

Leave it behind.
Take your head out of your hands
and arise from the couch of melancholy
where the window-light falls against your face
and the sun rides across the autumn sky,
steely behind the bare trees,
glorious as the high strains of violins.

But forget Strauss.
And forget his younger brother,
the poor bastard who was killed in a fall
from a podium while conducting a symphony.

Forget the past,
forget the stunned audience on its feet,
the absurdity of their formal clothes
in the face of sudden death,
forget their collective gasp,
the murmur and huddle over the body,
the creaking of the lowered curtain.

Forget Strauss
with that encore look in his eye
and his tiresome industry:
more than five hundred finished compositions!
He even wrote a polka for his mother.
That alone is enough to make me flee the past,
evacuate its temples,
and walk alone under the stars
down these dark paths strewn with acorns,
feeling nothing but the crisp October air,
the swing of my arms
and the rhythm of my stepping—
a man of the present who has forgotten
every composer, every great battle,
just me,
a thin reed blowing in the night.

Picnic, Lightning

(1 9 9 8)

Fishing on the Susquehanna in July

I have never been fishing on the Susquehanna
or on any river for that matter
to be perfectly honest.

Not in July or any month
have I had the pleasure—if it is a pleasure—
of fishing on the Susquehanna.

I am more likely to be found
in a quiet room like this one—
a painting of a woman on the wall,

a bowl of tangerines on the table—
trying to manufacture the sensation
of fishing on the Susquehanna.

There is little doubt
that others have been fishing
on the Susquehanna,

rowing upstream in a wooden boat,
sliding the oars under the water
then raising them to drip in the light.

But the nearest I have ever come to
fishing on the Susquehanna
was one afternoon in a museum in Philadelphia

when I balanced a little egg of time
in front of a painting
in which that river curled around a bend

under a blue cloud-ruffled sky,
dense trees along the banks,
and a fellow with a red bandanna

sitting in a small, green
flat-bottom boat
holding the thin whip of a pole.

That is something I am unlikely
ever to do, I remember
saying to myself and the person next to me.

Then I blinked and moved on
to other American scenes
of haystacks, water whitening over rocks,

even one of a brown hare
who seemed so wired with alertness
I imagined him springing right out of the frame.

To a Stranger Born in Some Distant Country
Hundreds of Years from Now

> *I write poems for a stranger who will be born in some*
> *distant country hundreds of years from now.*
> —*Mary Oliver*

Nobody here likes a wet dog.
No one wants anything to do with a dog
that is wet from being out in the rain
or retrieving a stick from a lake.
Look how she wanders around the crowded pub tonight
going from one person to another
hoping for a pat on the head, a rub behind the ears,
something that could be given with one hand
without even wrinkling the conversation.

But everyone pushes her away,
some with a knee, others with the sole of a boot.
Even the children, who don't realize she is wet
until they go to pet her,
push her away
then wipe their hands on their clothes.
And whenever she heads toward me,
I show her my palm, and she turns aside.

O stranger of the future!
O inconceivable being!
whatever the shape of your house,
however you scoot from place to place,
no matter how strange and colorless the clothes you
    may wear,
I bet nobody there likes a wet dog either.
I bet everybody in your pub,
even the children, pushes her away.

I Chop Some Parsley While Listening to Art Blakey's Version of "Three Blind Mice"

And I start wondering how they came to be blind.
If it was congenital, they could be brothers and sisters,
and I think of the poor mother
brooding over her sightless young triplets.

Or was it a common accident, all three caught
in a searing explosion, a firework perhaps?
If not,
if each came to his or her blindness separately,

how did they ever manage to find one another?
Would it not be difficult for a blind mouse
to locate even one fellow mouse with vision
let alone two other blind ones?

And how, in their tiny darkness,
could they possibly have run after a farmer's wife
or anyone else's wife for that matter?
Not to mention why.

Just so she could cut off their tails
with a carving knife, is the cynic's answer,
but the thought of them without eyes
and now without tails to trail through the moist grass

or slip around the corner of a baseboard
has the cynic who always lounges within me
up off his couch and at the window
trying to hide the rising softness that he feels.

By now I am on to dicing an onion

which might account for the wet stinging
in my own eyes, though Freddie Hubbard's
mournful trumpet on "Blue Moon,"

which happens to be the next cut,
cannot be said to be making matters any better.

Afternoon with Irish Cows

There were a few dozen who occupied the field
across the road from where we lived,
stepping all day from tuft to tuft,
their big heads down in the soft grass,
though I would sometimes pass a window
and look out to see the field suddenly empty
as if they had taken wing, flown off to another country.

Then later, I would open the blue front door,
and again the field would be full of their munching,
or they would be lying down
on the black-and-white maps of their sides,
facing in all directions, waiting for rain.
How mysterious, how patient and dumbfounded
they appeared in the long quiet of the afternoons.

But every once in a while, one of them
would let out a sound so phenomenal
that I would put down the paper
or the knife I was cutting an apple with
and walk across the road to the stone wall
to see which one of them was being torched
or pierced through the side with a long spear.

Yes, it sounded like pain until I could see
the noisy one, anchored there on all fours,
her neck outstretched, her bellowing head
laboring upward as she gave voice
to the rising, full-bodied cry
that began in the darkness of her belly
and echoed up through her bowed ribs into her
    gaping mouth.

Then I knew that she was only announcing
the large, unadulterated cowness of herself,
pouring out the ancient apologia of her kind
to all the green fields and the gray clouds,
to the limestone hills and the inlet of the blue bay,
while she regarded my head and shoulders
above the wall with one wild, shocking eye.

Marginalia

Sometimes the notes are ferocious,
skirmishes against the author
raging along the borders of every page
in tiny black script.
If I could just get my hands on you,
Kierkegaard, or Conor Cruise O'Brien,
they seem to say,
I would bolt the door and beat some logic into your head.

Other comments are more offhand, dismissive—
"Nonsense." "Please!" "HA!!"—
that kind of thing.
I remember once looking up from my reading,
my thumb as a bookmark,
trying to imagine what the person must look like
who wrote "Don't be a ninny"
alongside a paragraph in *The Life of Emily Dickinson*.

Students are more modest
needing to leave only their splayed footprints
along the shore of the page.
One scrawls "Metaphor" next to a stanza of Eliot's.
Another notes the presence of "Irony"
fifty times outside the paragraphs of *A Modest Proposal*.

Or they are fans who cheer from the empty bleachers,
hands cupped around their mouths.
"Absolutely," they shout
to Duns Scotus and James Baldwin.
"Yes." "Bull's-eye." "My man!"
Check marks, asterisks, and exclamation points
rain down along the sidelines.

And if you have managed to graduate from college
without ever having written "Man vs. Nature"
in a margin, perhaps now
is the time to take one step forward.

We have all seized the white perimeter as our own
and reached for a pen if only to show
we did not just laze in an armchair turning pages;
we pressed a thought into the wayside,
planted an impression along the verge.

Even Irish monks in their cold scriptoria
jotted along the borders of the Gospels
brief asides about the pains of copying,
a bird singing near their window,
or the sunlight that illuminated their page—
anonymous men catching a ride into the future
on a vessel more lasting than themselves.

And you have not read Joshua Reynolds,
they say, until you have read him
enwreathed with Blake's furious scribbling.

Yet the one I think of most often,
the one that dangles from me like a locket,
was written in the copy of *Catcher in the Rye*
I borrowed from the local library
one slow, hot summer.
I was just beginning high school then,
reading books on a davenport in my parents' living room,
and I cannot tell you
how vastly my loneliness was deepened,

how poignant and amplified the world before me seemed,
when I found on one page

a few greasy looking smears
and next to them, written in soft pencil—
by a beautiful girl, I could tell,
whom I would never meet—
"Pardon the egg salad stains, but I'm in love."

Some Days

Some days I put the people in their places at the table,
bend their legs at the knees,
if they come with that feature,
and fix them into the tiny wooden chairs.

All afternoon they face one another,
the man in the brown suit,
the woman in the blue dress,
perfectly motionless, perfectly behaved.

But other days, I am the one
who is lifted up by the ribs,
then lowered into the dining room of a dollhouse
to sit with the others at the long table.

Very funny,
but how would you like it
if you never knew from one day to the next
if you were going to spend it

striding around like a vivid god,
your shoulders in the clouds,
or sitting down there amidst the wallpaper,
staring straight ahead with your little plastic face?

Picnic, Lightning

My very photogenic mother died in a freak accident
(picnic, lightning) when I was three.

—Lolita

It is possible to be struck by a meteor
or a single-engine plane
while reading in a chair at home.
Safes drop from rooftops
and flatten the odd pedestrian
mostly within the panels of the comics,
but still, we know it is possible,
as well as the flash of summer lightning,
the thermos toppling over,
spilling out on the grass.

And we know the message
can be delivered from within.
The heart, no valentine,
decides to quit after lunch,
the power shut off like a switch,
or a tiny dark ship is unmoored
into the flow of the body's rivers,
the brain a monastery,
defenseless on the shore.

This is what I think about
when I shovel compost
into a wheelbarrow,
and when I fill the long flower boxes,
then press into rows

the limp roots of red impatiens—
the instant hand of Death
always ready to burst forth
from the sleeve of his voluminous cloak.

Then the soil is full of marvels,
bits of leaf like flakes off a fresco,
red-brown pine needles, a beetle quick
to burrow back under the loam.
Then the wheelbarrow is a wilder blue,
the clouds a brighter white,

and all I hear is the rasp of the steel edge
against a round stone,
the small plants singing
with lifted faces, and the click
of the sundial
as one hour sweeps into the next.

Morning

Why do we bother with the rest of the day,
the swale of the afternoon,
the sudden dip into evening,

then night with his notorious perfumes,
his many-pointed stars?

This is the best—
throwing off the light covers,
feet on the cold floor,
and buzzing around the house on espresso—

maybe a splash of water on the face,
a palmful of vitamins—
but mostly buzzing around the house on espresso,

dictionary and atlas open on the rug,
the typewriter waiting for the key of the head,
a cello on the radio,

and, if necessary, the windows—
trees fifty, a hundred years old
out there,
heavy clouds on the way
and the lawn steaming like a horse
in the early morning.

Bonsai

All it takes is one to throw a room
completely out of whack.

Over by the window
it looks hundreds of yards away,

a lone stark gesture of wood
on the distant cliff of a table.

Up close, it draws you in,
cuts everything down to its size.

Look at it from the doorway,
and the world dilates and bloats.

The button lying next to it
is now a pearl wheel,

the book of matches is a raft,
and the coffee cup a cistern

to catch the same rain
that moistens its small plot of dark, mossy earth.

For it even carries its own weather,
leaning away from a fierce wind

that somehow blows
through the calm tropics of this room.

The way it bends inland at the elbow
makes me want to inch my way

to the very top of its spiky greenery,
hold on for dear life

and watch the sea storm rage,
hoping for a tiny whale to appear.

I want to see her plunging forward
through the troughs,

tunneling under the foam and spindrift
on her annual, thousand-mile journey.

Shoveling Snow with Buddha

In the usual iconography of the temple or the local Wok
you would never see him doing such a thing,
tossing the dry snow over the mountain
of his bare, round shoulder,
his hair tied in a knot,
a model of concentration.

Sitting is more his speed, if that is the word
for what he does, or does not do.

Even the season is wrong for him.
In all his manifestations, is it not warm and slightly humid?
Is this not implied by his serene expression,
that smile so wide it wraps itself around the waist of the
    universe?

But here we are, working our way down the driveway,
one shovelful at a time.
We toss the light powder into the clear air.
We feel the cold mist on our faces.
And with every heave we disappear
and become lost to each other
in these sudden clouds of our own making,
these fountain-bursts of snow.

This is so much better than a sermon in church,
I say out loud, but Buddha keeps on shoveling.
This is the true religion, the religion of snow,
and sunlight and winter geese barking in the sky,
I say, but he is too busy to hear me.

He has thrown himself into shoveling snow
as if it were the purpose of existence,
as if the sign of a perfect life were a clear driveway
you could back the car down easily
and drive off into the vanities of the world
with a broken heater fan and a song on the radio.

All morning long we work side by side,
me with my commentary
and he inside the generous pocket of his silence,
until the hour is nearly noon
and the snow is piled high all around us;
then, I hear him speak.

After this, he asks,
can we go inside and play cards?

Certainly, I reply, and I will heat some milk
and bring cups of hot chocolate to the table
while you shuffle the deck,
and our boots stand dripping by the door.

Aaah, says the Buddha, lifting his eyes
and leaning for a moment on his shovel
before he drives the thin blade again
deep into the glittering white snow.

Snow

I cannot help noticing how this slow Monk solo
seems to go somehow
with the snow
that is coming down this morning,

how the notes and the spaces accompany
its easy falling
on the geometry of the ground,
on the flagstone path,
the slanted roof,
and the angles of the split-rail fence

as if he had imagined a winter scene
as he sat at the piano
late one night at the Five Spot
playing "Ruby, My Dear."

Then again, it's the kind of song
that would go easily with rain
or a tumult of leaves,

and for that matter it's a snow
that could attend
an adagio for strings,
the best of the Ronettes,
or George Thorogood and the Destroyers.

It falls so indifferently
into the spacious white parlor of the world,
if I were sitting here reading

in silence,
reading the morning paper
or reading *Being and Nothingness*,
not even letting the spoon
touch the inside of the cup,
I have a feeling
the snow would even go perfectly with that.

Japan

Today I pass the time reading
a favorite haiku,
saying the few words over and over.

It feels like eating
the same small, perfect grape
again and again.

I walk through the house reciting it
and leave its letters falling
through the air of every room.

I stand by the big silence of the piano and say it.
I say it in front of a painting of the sea.
I tap out its rhythm on an empty shelf.

I listen to myself saying it,
then I say it without listening,
then I hear it without saying it.

And when the dog looks up at me,
I kneel down on the floor
and whisper it into each of his long white ears.

It's the one about the one-ton
temple bell
with the moth sleeping on its surface,

and every time I say it, I feel the excruciating
pressure of the moth
on the surface of the iron bell.

When I say it at the window,
the bell is the world
and I am the moth resting there.

When I say it into the mirror,
I am the heavy bell
and the moth is life with its papery wings.

And later, when I say it to you in the dark,
you are the bell,
and I am the tongue of the bell, ringing you,

and the moth has flown
from its line
and moves like a hinge in the air above our bed.

Victoria's Secret

The one in the upper left-hand corner
is giving me a look
that says I know you are here
and I have nothing better to do
for the remainder of human time
than return your persistent but engaging stare.
She is wearing a deeply scalloped
flame-stitch halter top
with padded push-up styling
and easy side-zip tap pants.

The one on the facing page, however,
who looks at me over her bare shoulder,
cannot hide the shadow of annoyance in her brow.
You have interrupted me,
she seems to be saying,
with your coughing and your loud music.
Now please leave me alone;
let me finish whatever it was I was doing
in my organza-trimmed
whisperweight camisole with
keyhole closure and a point d'esprit mesh back.

I wet my thumb and flip the page.
Here, the one who happens to be reclining
in a satin and lace merry widow
with an inset lace-up front,
decorated underwire cups and bodice
with lace ruffles along the bottom

and hook-and-eye closure in the back,
is wearing a slightly contorted expression,
her head thrust back, mouth partially open,
a confusing mixture of pain and surprise
as if she had stepped on a tack
just as I was breaking down
her bedroom door with my shoulder.

Nor does the one directly beneath her
look particularly happy to see me.
She is arching one eyebrow slightly
as if to say, so what if I am wearing nothing
but this stretch panne velvet bodysuit
with a low sweetheart neckline
featuring molded cups and adjustable straps.
Do you have a problem with that?!

The one on the far right is easier to take,
her eyes half-closed
as if she were listening to a medley
of lullabies playing faintly on a music box.
Soon she will drop off to sleep,
her head nestled in the soft crook of her arm,
and later she will wake up in her
Spandex slip dress with the high side slit,
deep scoop neckline, elastic shirring,
and concealed back zip and vent.

But opposite her,
stretched out catlike on a couch
in the warm glow of a paneled library,

is one who wears a distinctly challenging expression,
her face tipped up, exposing
her long neck, her perfectly flared nostrils.
Go ahead, her expression tells me,
take off my satin charmeuse gown
with a sheer, jacquard bodice
decorated with a touch of shimmering Lurex.
Go ahead, fling it into the fireplace.
What do I care, her eyes say, we're all going to hell anyway.

I have other mail to open,
but I cannot help noticing her neighbor
whose eyes are downcast,
her head ever so demurely bowed to the side
as if she were the model who sat for Correggio
when he painted "The Madonna of St. Jerome,"
only it became so ungodly hot in Parma
that afternoon, she had to remove
the traditional blue robe
and pose there in his studio
in a beautifully shaped satin teddy
with an embossed V-front,
princess seaming to mold the bodice,
and puckered knit detail.

And occupying the whole facing page
is one who displays that expression
we have come to associate with photographic beauty.
Yes, she is pouting about something,
all lower lip and cheekbone.
Perhaps her ice cream has tumbled

out of its cone onto the parquet floor.
Perhaps she has been waiting all day
for a new sofa to be delivered,
waiting all day in a stretch lace hipster
with lattice edging, satin frog closures,
velvet scrollwork, cuffed ankles,
flare silhouette, and knotted shoulder straps
available in black, champagne, almond,
cinnabar, plum, bronze, mocha,
peach, ivory, caramel, blush, butter, rose, and periwinkle.
It is, of course, impossible to say,
impossible to know what she is thinking,
why her mouth is the shape of petulance.

But this is already too much.
Who has the time to linger on these delicate
lures, these once unmentionable things?
Life is rushing by like a mad, swollen river.
One minute roses are opening in the garden
and the next, snow is flying past my window.
Plus the phone is ringing.
The dog is whining at the door.
Rain is beating on the roof.
And as always there is a list of things I have to do
before the night descends, black and silky,
and the dark hours begin to hurtle by,
before the little doors of the body swing shut
and I ride to sleep, my closed eyes
still burning from all the glossy lights of day.

Lines Composed Over Three Thousand Miles from Tintern Abbey

I was here before, a long time ago,
and now I am here again
is an observation that occurs in poetry
as frequently as rain occurs in life.

The fellow may be gazing
over an English landscape,
hillsides dotted with sheep,
a row of tall trees topping the downs,

or he could be moping through the shadows
of a dark Bavarian forest,
a wedge of cheese and a volume of fairy tales
tucked into his rucksack.

But the feeling is always the same.
It was better the first time.
This time is not nearly as good.
I'm not feeling as chipper as I did back then.

Something is always missing—
swans, a glint on the surface of a lake,
some minor but essential touch.
Or the quality of things has diminished.

The sky was a deeper, more dimensional blue,
clouds were more cathedral-like,
and water rushed over rock
with greater effervescence.

From our chairs we have watched
the poor author in his waistcoat
as he recalls the dizzying icebergs of childhood
and mills around in a field of weeds.

We have heard the poets long dead
declaim their dying
from a promontory, a riverbank,
next to a haycock, within a copse.

We have listened to their dismay,
the kind that issues from poems
the way water issues forth from hoses,
the way the match always gives its little speech on fire.

And when we put down the book at last,
lean back, close our eyes,
stinging with print,
and slip in the bookmark of sleep,

we will be schooled enough to know
that when we wake up
a little before dinner
things will not be nearly as good as they once were.

Something will be missing
from this long, coffin-shaped room,
the walls and windows now
only two different shades of gray,

the glossy gardenia drooping
in its chipped terra-cotta pot.
And on the floor, shoes, socks,
the browning core of an apple.

Nothing will be as it was
a few hours ago, back in the glorious past
before our naps, back in that Golden Age
that drew to a close sometime shortly after lunch.

Paradelle for Susan

I remember the quick, nervous bird of your love.
I remember the quick, nervous bird of your love.
Always perched on the thinnest, highest branch.
Always perched on the thinnest, highest branch.
Thinnest love, remember the quick branch.
Always nervous, I perched on your highest bird the.

It is time for me to cross the mountain.
It is time for me to cross the mountain.
And find another shore to darken with my pain.
And find another shore to darken with my pain.
Another pain for me to darken the mountain.
And find the time, cross my shore, to with it is to.

The weather warm, the handwriting familiar.
The weather warm, the handwriting familiar.
Your letter flies from my hand into the waters below.
Your letter flies from my hand into the waters below.
The familiar waters below my warm hand.
Into handwriting your weather flies you letter the from the.

I always cross the highest letter, the thinnest bird.
Below the waters of my warm familiar pain,
Another hand to remember your handwriting.
The weather perched for me on the shore.
Quick, your nervous branch flew from love.
Darken the mountain, time and find was my into it
    was with to to.

NOTE: The paradelle is one of the more demanding French fixed forms, first appearing in the langue d'oc love poetry of the eleventh century. It is a poem of four six-line stanzas in which the first and second lines, as well as the third and fourth lines of the first three stanzas, must be identical. The fifth and sixth lines, which traditionally resolve these stanzas, must use *all* the words from the preceding lines and *only* those words. Similarly, the final stanza must use *every* word from *all* the preceding stanzas and *only* those words.

Lines Lost Among Trees

These are not the lines that came to me
while walking in the woods
with no pen
and nothing to write on anyway.

They are gone forever,
a handful of coins
dropped through the grate of memory,
along with the ingenious mnemonic

I devised to hold them in place—
all gone and forgotten
before I had returned to the clearing of lawn
in back of our quiet house

with its jars jammed with pens,
its notebooks and reams of blank paper,
its desk and soft lamp,
its table and the light from its windows.

So this is my elegy for them,
those six or eight exhalations,
the braided rope of the syntax,
the jazz of the timing,

and the little insight at the end
wagging like the short tail
of a perfectly obedient spaniel
sitting by the door.

This is my envoy to nothing
where I say Go, little poem—
not out into the world of strangers' eyes,
but off to some airy limbo,

home to lost epics,
unremembered names,
and fugitive dreams
such as the one I had last night,

which, like a fantastic city in pencil,
erased itself
in the bright morning air
just as I was waking up.

Taking Off Emily Dickinson's Clothes

First, her tippet made of tulle,
easily lifted off her shoulders and laid
on the back of a wooden chair.

And her bonnet,
the bow undone with a light forward pull.

Then the long white dress, a more
complicated matter with mother-of-pearl
buttons down the back,
so tiny and numerous that it takes forever
before my hands can part the fabric,
like a swimmer's dividing water,
and slip inside.

You will want to know
that she was standing
by an open window in an upstairs bedroom,
motionless, a little wide-eyed,
looking out at the orchard below,
the white dress puddled at her feet
on the wide-board, hardwood floor.

The complexity of women's undergarments
in nineteenth-century America
is not to be waved off,
and I proceeded like a polar explorer
through clips, clasps, and moorings,
catches, straps, and whalebone stays,
sailing toward the iceberg of her nakedness.

Later, I wrote in a notebook
it was like riding a swan into the night,
but, of course, I cannot tell you everything—
the way she closed her eyes to the orchard,
how her hair tumbled free of its pins,
how there were sudden dashes
whenever we spoke.

What I can tell you is
it was terribly quiet in Amherst
that Sabbath afternoon,
nothing but a carriage passing the house,
a fly buzzing in a windowpane.

So I could plainly hear her inhale
when I undid the very top
hook-and-eye fastener of her corset

and I could hear her sigh when finally it was unloosed,
the way some readers sigh when they realize
that Hope has feathers,
that Reason is a plank,
that Life is a loaded gun
that looks right at you with a yellow eye.

The Night House

Every day the body works in the fields of the world
mending a stone wall
or swinging a sickle through the tall grass—
the grass of civics, the grass of money—
and every night the body curls around itself
and listens for the soft bells of sleep.

But the heart is restless and rises
from the body in the middle of the night,
leaves the trapezoidal bedroom
with its thick, pictureless walls
to sit by herself at the kitchen table
and heat some milk in a pan.

And the mind gets up too, puts on a robe
and goes downstairs, lights a cigarette,
and opens a book on engineering.
Even the conscience awakens
and roams from room to room in the dark,
darting away from every mirror like a strange fish.

And the soul is up on the roof
in her nightdress, straddling the ridge,
singing a song about the wildness of the sea
until the first rip of pink appears in the sky.
Then, they all will return to the sleeping body
the way a flock of birds settles back into a tree,

resuming their daily colloquy,
talking to each other or themselves
even through the heat of the long afternoons.

Which is why the body—that house of voices—
sometimes puts down its metal tongs, its needle, or its pen
to stare into the distance,

to listen to all its names being called
before bending again to its labor.

Splitting Wood

Frost covered this decades ago,
and frost will cover it again tonight,
the leafy disarray of this woodland

now thinned down to half its trees,
but this morning I stand here
sweating in a thin shirt

as I split a stack of ash logs
into firewood
with two wedges, an ax, and a blue-headed maul.

The pleasures here are well known:
the feet planted wide,
the silent unstoppable flow of the downswing,

the coordination that is called hand-eye,
because the hand achieves
whatever the concupiscent eye desires

when it longs for a certain spot,
which, in this case, is the slightest fissure
visible at one end of the log

where the thin, insinuating edge
of the blade can gain entry,
where the shape of its will can be done.

I want to say there is nothing
like the sudden opening of wood,
but it is like so many other things—

the stroke of the ax like lightning,
the bisection so perfect
the halves fall away from each other

as in a mirror,
and hit the soft ground
like twins shot through the heart.

And rarely, if the wood
accepts the blade without conditions,
the two pieces keep their balance

in spite of the blow,
remain stunned on the block
as if they cannot believe their division,

their sudden separateness.
Still upright, still together,
they wobble slightly

as two lovers, once secretly bound,
might stand revealed,
more naked than ever,

the darkness inside the tree they shared
now instantly exposed to the blunt
light of this clear November day,

all the inner twisting of the grain
that held them blindly
in their augmentation and contortion

now rushed into this brightness
as if by a shutter
that, once opened, can never be closed.

The Death of the Hat

Once every man wore a hat.

In the ashen newsreels,
the avenues of cities
are broad rivers flowing with hats.

The ballparks swelled
with thousands of straw hats,
brims and bands,
rows of men smoking
and cheering in shirtsleeves.

Hats were the law.
They went without saying.
You noticed a man without a hat in a crowd.

You bought them from Adams or Dobbs
who branded your initials in gold
on the inside band.

Trolleys crisscrossed the city.
Steamships sailed in and out of the harbor.
Men with hats gathered on the docks.

There was a person to block your hat
and a hatcheck girl to mind it
while you had a drink
or ate a steak with peas and a baked potato.
In your office stood a hat rack.

The day war was declared
everyone in the street was wearing a hat.
And they were wearing hats
when a ship loaded with men sank in the icy sea.

My father wore one to work every day
and returned home
carrying the evening paper,
the winter chill radiating from his overcoat.

But today we go bareheaded
into the winter streets,
stand hatless on frozen platforms.

Today the mailboxes on the roadside
and the spruce trees behind the house
wear cold white hats of snow.

Mice scurry from the stone walls at night
in their thin fur hats
to eat the birdseed that has spilled.

And now my father, after a life of work,
wears a hat of earth,
and on top of that,
a lighter one of cloud and sky—a hat of wind.

Passengers

At the gate, I sit in a row of blue seats
with the possible company of my death,
this sprawling miscellany of people—
carry-on bags and paperbacks—

that could be gathered in a flash
into a band of pilgrims on the last open road.
Not that I think
if our plane crumpled into a mountain

we would all ascend together,
holding hands like a ring of sky divers,
into a sudden gasp of brightness,
or that there would be some common spot

for us to reunite to jubilize the moment,
some spaceless, pillarless Greece
where we could, at the count of three,
toss our ashes into the sunny air.

It's just that the way that man has his briefcase
so carefully arranged,
the way that girl is cooling her tea,
and the flow of the comb that woman

passes through her daughter's hair . . .
and when you consider the altitude,
the secret parts of the engines,
and all the hard water and the deep canyons below . . .

well, I just think it would be good if one of us
maybe stood up and said a few words,
or, so as not to involve the police,
at least quietly wrote something down.

Where I Live

The house sits at one end of a two-acre trapezoid.
There is a wide lawn, a long brick path,
rhododendrons, and large, heavy maples.

Behind the geometry of the nine rooms,
the woods run up a hillside;
and across the road in front

is a stream called the Plum Brook.
It must have flowed through an orchard
that no longer exists.

Tomorrow early, I will drive down
and talk to the stonecutter,
but today I am staying home,

standing at one window, then another,
or putting on a jacket
and wandering around outside

or sitting in a chair
watching the trees full of light-green buds
under the low hood of the sky.

This is the first good rain to fall
since my father was buried last week,
and even though he was very old,

I am amazed at how the small drops
stream down the panes of glass,
as usual,

gathering,
as they always have,
in pools on the ground.

Aristotle

This is the beginning.
Almost anything can happen.
This is where you find
the creation of light, a fish wriggling onto land,
the first word of *Paradise Lost* on an empty page.
Think of an egg, the letter *A,*
a woman ironing on a bare stage
as the heavy curtain rises.
This is the very beginning.
The first-person narrator introduces himself,
tells us about his lineage.
The mezzo-soprano stands in the wings.
Here the climbers are studying a map
or pulling on their long woolen socks.
This is early on, years before the Ark, dawn.
The profile of an animal is being smeared
on the wall of a cave,
and you have not yet learned to crawl.
This is the opening, the gambit,
a pawn moving forward an inch.
This is your first night with her,
your first night without her.
This is the first part
where the wheels begin to turn,
where the elevator begins its ascent,
before the doors lurch apart.

This is the middle.
Things have had time to get complicated,
messy, really. Nothing is simple anymore.
Cities have sprouted up along the rivers

teeming with people at cross-purposes—
a million schemes, a million wild looks.
Disappointment unshoulders his knapsack
here and pitches his ragged tent.
This is the sticky part where the plot congeals,
where the action suddenly reverses
or swerves off in an outrageous direction.
Here the narrator devotes a long paragraph
to why Miriam does not want Edward's child.
Someone hides a letter under a pillow.
Here the aria rises to a pitch,
a song of betrayal, salted with revenge.
And the climbing party is stuck on a ledge
halfway up the mountain.
This is the bridge, the painful modulation.
This is the thick of things.
So much is crowded into the middle—
the guitars of Spain, piles of ripe avocados,
Russian uniforms, noisy parties,
lakeside kisses, arguments heard through a wall—
too much to name, too much to think about.

And this is the end,
the car running out of road,
the river losing its name in an ocean,
the long nose of the photographed horse
touching the white electronic line.
This is the colophon, the last elephant in the parade,
the empty wheelchair,
and pigeons floating down in the evening.
Here the stage is littered with bodies,

the narrator leads the characters to their cells,
and the climbers are in their graves.
It is me hitting the period
and you closing the book.
It is Sylvia Plath in the kitchen
and St. Clement with an anchor around his neck.
This is the final bit
thinning away to nothing.
This is the end, according to Aristotle,
what we have all been waiting for,
what everything comes down to,
the destination we cannot help imagining,
a streak of light in the sky,
a hat on a peg, and outside the cabin, falling leaves.

New Poems

Dharma

The way the dog trots out the front door
every morning
without a hat or an umbrella,
without any money
or the keys to her doghouse
never fails to fill the saucer of my heart
with milky admiration.

Who provides a finer example
of a life without encumbrance—
Thoreau in his curtainless hut
with a single plate, a single spoon?
Gandhi with his staff and his holy diapers?

Off she goes into the material world
with nothing but her brown coat
and her modest blue collar,
following only her wet nose,
the twin portals of her steady breathing,
followed only by the plume of her tail.

If only she did not shove the cat aside
every morning
and eat all his food
what a model of self-containment she would be,
what a paragon of earthly detachment.
If only she were not so eager
for a rub behind the ears,
so acrobatic in her welcomes,
if only I were not her god.

Reading an Anthology of Chinese Poems of the Sung Dynasty, I Pause to Admire the Length and Clarity of Their Titles

It seems these poets have nothing
up their ample sleeves
they turn over so many cards so early,
telling us before the first line
whether it is wet or dry,
night or day, the season the man is standing in,
even how much he has had to drink.

Maybe it is autumn and he is looking at a sparrow.
Maybe it is snowing on a town with a beautiful name.

"Viewing Peonies at the Temple of Good Fortune
on a Cloudy Afternoon" is one of Sun Tung Po's.
"Dipping Water from the River and Simmering Tea"
is another one, or just
"On a Boat, Awake at Night."

And Lu Yu takes the simple rice cake with
"In a Boat on a Summer Evening
I Heard the Cry of a Waterbird.
It Was Very Sad and Seemed to be Saying
My Woman Is Cruel—Moved, I Wrote This Poem"

There is no iron turnstile to push against here
as with headings like "Vortex on a String,"
"The Horn of Neurosis," or whatever.
No confusingly inscribed welcome mat to puzzle over.

Instead, "I Walk Out on a Summer Morning
to the Sound of Birds and a Waterfall"
is a beaded curtain brushing over my shoulders.

And "Ten Days of Spring Rain Have Kept Me Indoors"
is a servant who shows me into the room
where a poet with a thin beard
is sitting on a mat with a jug of wine
whispering something about clouds and cold wind,
about sickness and the loss of friends

How easy he has made it for me to enter here,
to sit down in a corner;
cross my legs like his, and listen.

Snow Day

Today we woke up to a revolution of snow,
its white flag waving over everything,
the landscape vanished,
not a single mouse to punctuate the blankness,
and beyond these windows

the government buildings smothered,
schools and libraries buried, the post office lost
under the noiseless drift,
the paths of trains softly blocked,
the world fallen under this falling.

In a while, I will put on some boots
and step out like someone walking in water,
and the dog will porpoise through the drifts,
and I will shake a laden branch
sending a cold shower down on us both.

But for now I am a willing prisoner in this house,
a sympathizer with the anarchic cause of snow.
I will make a pot of tea
and listen to the plastic radio on the counter,
as glad as anyone to hear the news

that the Kiddie Corner School is closed,
the Ding-Dong School, closed.
the All Aboard Children's School, closed,
the Hi-Ho Nursery School, closed,
along with—some will be delighted to hear—

the Toadstool School, the Little School,
Little Sparrows Nursery School,
Little Stars Pre-School, Peas-and-Carrots Day School
the Tom Thumb Child Center, all closed,
and—clap your hands—the Peanuts Play School.

So this is where the children hide all day,
These are the nests where they letter and draw,
where they put on their bright miniature jackets,
all darting and climbing and sliding,
all but the few girls whispering by the fence.

And now I am listening hard
in the grandiose silence of the snow,
trying to hear what those three girls are plotting,
what riot is afoot,
which small queen is about to be brought down.

Insomnia

Even though the house is deeply silent
and the room, with no moon,
is perfectly dark,
even though the body is a sack of exhaustion
inert on the bed,

someone inside me will not
get off his tricycle,
will not stop tracing the same tight circle
on the same green threadbare carpet.

It makes no difference whether I lie
staring at the ceiling
or pace the living-room floor,
he keeps on making his furious rounds,
little pedaler in his frenzy,
my own worst enemy, my oldest friend.

What is there to do but close my eyes
and watch him circling the night,
schoolboy in an ill-fitting jacket,
leaning forward, his cap on backwards,
wringing the handlebars,
maintaining a certain speed?

Does anything exist at this hour
in this nest of dark rooms
but the spectacle of him
and the hope that before dawn

I can lift out some curious detail
that will carry me off to sleep—
the watch that encircles his pale wrist,
the expandable band,
the tiny hands that keep pointing this way and that.

Madmen

They say you can jinx a poem
if you talk about it before it is done.
If you let it out too early, they warn,
your poem will fly away,
and this time they are absolutely right.

Take the night I mentioned to you
I wanted to write about the madmen,
as the newspapers so blithely call them,
who attack art, not in reviews,
but with breadknives and hammers
in the quiet museums of Prague and Amsterdam.

Actually, they are the real artists,
you said, spinning the ice in your glass.
The screwdriver is their brush.
The restorers are the true vandals,
you went on, slowly turning me upside-down,
the ones in the white smocks
always closing the wound in the landscape
and ruining the art of the mad.

I watched my poem fly down to the front
of the bar and hover there
until the next customer walked in—
then I watched it fly out the door into the night
and sail away, I could only imagine,
over the dark tenements of the city.

All I had wished to say
was that art, too, was short,

as a razor can teach with a blind slash;
it only seems long when you compare it to life,
but that night I drove home alone
with nothing swinging in the cage of my heart
but the faint hope that I might catch
in the fan of my headlights
a glimpse of the thing,
maybe perched on a road sign or a streetlamp—
poor unwritten bird, its wings folded,
staring down at me with tiny illuminated eyes.

Sonnet

All we need is fourteen lines, well, thirteen now,
and after this one just a dozen
to launch a little ship on love's storm-tossed seas,
then only ten more left like rows of beans.
How easily it goes unless you get Elizabethan
and insist the iambic bongos must be played
and rhymes positioned at the ends of lines,
one for every station of the cross.
But hang on here while we make the turn
into the final six where all will be resolved,
where longing and heartache will find an end,
where Laura will tell Petrarch to put down his pen,
take off those crazy medieval tights,
blow out the lights, and come at last to bed.

Idiomatic

It is a big question to pose so early in the morning
or "in the light woven by birds,"
as the Estonians say,
but still I must ask what is my place in life?
my "seat on the invisible train,"
as they say in Hungary.
I mean why am I just sitting here
in a lawn chair listening to a thrush,
"the little entertainer of the woods,"
as the Swiss call him,
while out there in the world
mobs of people are rushing over bridges
in and out of the cities?
Vegetables grow heavy in their fields,
clouds fly across the "face of the earth,"
as we call it in English,
and sometimes rockets lift off in the distance—
and I mean that quite literally,
"from the top of the table" as the Portuguese have it,
real rockets rising from the horizon,
or "the big line," if you're an Australian,
leaving behind rich gowns of exhaust smoke,
long, smooth trajectories,
and always the ocean below,
"the water machine," as the South Sea islanders put it—
everything taking place right on schedule,
"by the clock of the devil,"
as our grandparents were fond of saying.
And still here I sit with my shirt off,
the dog at my side, daydreaming—
"juggling balls of cotton," as they like to say in France.

The Waitress

She brings a drink to the table,
pivots, and turns away
with a smile

and soon she brings me
a menu, smiles,
and takes the empty glass away.

She brings me a fillet of sole
on a plate with parsley
and thin wheels of lemon,

then more bread in a basket,
smiling as she walks away,
then comes back

to see if everything is OK
to fill my glass with wine,
turning away

then circling back to my table
until she is every waitress
who has ever served me,

and every waiter, too,
young and old,
the eager and the sleepy ones alike.

I hold my fork in the air—
the blades of the fans
turn slowly on the ceiling—

and I begin to picture them all,
living and dead,
gathered together for one night

in an amphitheater, or armory
or some vast silvery ballroom
where they have come

to remove their bow ties,
to hang up their red jackets and aprons,
and now they are having a cigarette

or dancing with each other,
turning slowly in one another's arms
to a five-piece, rented band.

And that is all I can think about
after I pay the bill,
leave a large, sentimental tip,

then walk into the fluorescent streets,
collar up against the chill—
all the waitresses and waiters of my life,

until the night makes me realize
that this place where they pace and dance
under colored lights,

is made of nothing but autumn leaves,
red, yellow, gold,
waiting for a sudden gust of wind

to scatter it all
into the dark spaces
beyond these late-night, practically empty streets.

The Butterfly Effect

The one resting now on a plant stem
somewhere deep in the vine-hung
interior of South America
whose wings are about to flutter
thus causing it to rain heavily
on your wedding day
several years from now,
and spinning you down
a path to calamity and ruin
is—if it's any consolation—
a gorgeous swallowtail,
a brilliant mix of bright orange
and vivid yellow with a soft
dusting of light brown along the edges.

What's more, the two black dots
on the wings are so prominent
as to make one wonder
if this is not an example of mimicry,
an adaptation technique whereby one species
takes on the appearance
of another less-edible one,
first brought to light,
it might interest you to know
and possibly distract you from
your vexatious dread
with regards to the hopelessness of the future,
by two British naturalists, namely,
H. W. Bates in 1862 and A. R. Wallace in 1865.

Serenade

Let the other boys from the village
gather under your window
and strum their bean-shaped guitars.

Let them huddle under your balcony
heavy with flowers,
and fill the night with their longing—

locals in luminous shirts,
yodeling over their three simple chords,
hoping for a glimpse of your moonlit arm.

Meanwhile, I will bide my time
and continue my lessons on the zither
and my study of the miniature bassoon.

Every morning I will walk the corridor
to the music room
lined with the fierce portraits of my ancestors

knowing there is nothing like practice
to devour the hours of life—
sheets of music floating down,

a double reed in my mouth
or my fingers curled
over a row of wakeful strings.

And if this is not enough
to rouse you from your light sleep
and lure you through the open doors,

I will apply myself to the pyrophone,
the double-lap dulcimer,
the glassarina, and the tiny thumb piano.

I will be the strange one,
the pale eccentric
who wears the same clothes every day,

the one at the train station
carrying the black case
shaped like nothing you have seen before.

I will be the irresistible misfit
who sends up over a ledge of flowers
sounds no woman has ever heard—

the one who longs to see your face
framed by bougainvillea,
perplexed but full of charity,

looking down at me as I finger
a nameless instrument
it took so many days and nights to invent.

The Three Wishes

Because he has been hungry for days,
the woodsman wishes for a skillet of hot sausages
and because she is infuriated at his stupidity,
his lack of vision, shall we say,

his wife wishes the skillet would stick to his nose,
and so the last wish must also be squandered
by asking the genie to please
remove the heavy iron pan from the poor man's face.

Hovering in the smoke that wafts up
from his exotic green bottle,
the genie knew all along the couple
would never escape their miserable lot—

the cheerless hovel, the thin dog in the corner,
cold skillet on a cold stove—
and we knew this too, looking down from
the cloud of a sofa into the world of a book.

The man is a fool, it is easily said.
He could have wished for a million gold coins
as his wife will remind him hourly
for the rest of their rueful lives,

or a million golden skillets
if he had a little imaginative flair,
and that is the cinder of truth
the story wishes to place in one of our shoes.

Nothing can come from nothing,
I nod with the rest of the congregation.
Three wishes is three wishes too many,
I mutter piously as I look up from the story.

But every time I think of it,
all I ever really feel besides a quiver
of sympathy for the poor woodsman
is a gnawing hunger for sausages—

a sudden longing for a winter night,
a light snow falling outside,
my ax leaning by the door,
my devoted, heavyset wife at the stove,

and a skillet full of sizzling sausages,
maybe some green peppers and onions,
and for my seventh and final wish,
a decent bottle of Italian, no, wait . . . make that
    Chilean red.

Pavilion

I sit in the study,
simple walls, complicated design of carpet.
I read a book with a bright red cover.
I write something down.

I look up a fact in an encyclopedia
and copy it onto a card,
the lamp burning,
a painting leaning against a chair.

I find a word in a dictionary
and copy it onto the back of an envelope,
the piano heavy in the corner,
the fan turning slowly overhead.

Such is life in this pavilion
of paper and ink
where a cup of tea is cooling,
where the windows darken then fill with light.

But I have had enough of it—
the slope of paper on the desk,
books on the floor like water lilies,
the jasmine drying out in its pot.

In fact, I am ready to die,
ready to return as something else,
like a brown-and-white dog
with his head always out the car window.

Then maybe, if you were still around,
walking along a street in linen clothes,
a portfolio under your arm,
you would see me go by,

my eyes closed,
wet nose twitching,
my ears blown back,
a kind of smile on my long dark lips.

The Movies

I would like to watch a movie tonight
in which a stranger rides into town
or where someone embarks on a long journey,

a movie with the promise of danger,
danger visited upon the citizens of the town
by the stranger who rides in,

or the danger that will befall the person
on his or her long hazardous journey—
it hardly matters to me

so long as I am not in danger,
and not much danger lies in watching
a movie, you might as well agree.

I would prefer to watch this movie at home
than walk out in the cold to a theater
and stand on line for a ticket.

I want to watch it lying down
with the bed hitched up to the television
the way they'd hitch up a stagecoach

to a team of horses
so the movie could pull me along
the crooked, dusty road of its adventures.

I would stay out of harm's way
by identifying with characters
like the bartender in the movie about the stranger

who rides into town,
the fellow who knows enough to duck
when a chair shatters the mirror over the bar.

Or the stationmaster
in the movie about the perilous journey,
the fellow who fishes a gold watch from his pocket,

helps a lady onto the train,
and hands up a heavy satchel
to the man with the mustache

and the dangerous eyes,
waving the all-clear to the engineer.
Then the train would pull out of the station

and the movie would continue without me.
And at the end of the day
I would hang up my oval hat on a hook

and take the shortcut home to my two dogs,
my faithful, amorous wife, and my children—
Molly, Lucinda, and Harold, Jr.

Jealousy

It is not the tilted buildings or the blind alleys
that I mind,
nor the winding staircases leading nowhere
or the ones that are simply missing.

Nor is walking through a foreign city
with a ring of a thousand keys
looking for the one door the worst of it,
nor the blank maps I am offered by strangers.

I can even tolerate your constant running
away from me, slipping around corners,
rising in the cage of an elevator,
squinting out the rear window of a taxi,

and always on the arm of a tall man
in a beautiful suit
and a perfectly furled hat
whom I know is carrying a gun.

What kills me is the way you lie there
in the morning, eyes closed,
curled into a sweet ball of sleep
and that innocent look on your face

when you tell me over coffee and oranges
that really you were right there all night
next to me in bed
and then expect me to believe you

were lost in your own dreamworld,
some ridiculous alibi
involving swimming through clouds
to the pealing of bells,

a transparent white lie about leaping
from a high window ledge
then burying your face
in the plumage of an angel.

Tomes

There is a section in my library for death
and another for Irish history,
a few shelves for the poetry of China and Japan,
and in the center a row of reference books,
solid and imperturbable,
the ones you can turn to anytime,
when the night is going wrong
or when the day is full of empty promise.

I have nothing against
the thin monograph, the odd query,
a note on the identity of Chekhov's dentist—
but what I prefer on days like these
is to get up from the couch,
pull down *The History of the World,*
and hold in my hands a book
containing almost everything
and weighing no more than a sack of potatoes,
11 pounds, I discovered one day when I placed it
on the black iron scale
my mother used to keep in her kitchen,
the device on which she would place
a certain amount of flour,
a certain amount of fish.

Open flat on my lap
under a halo of lamplight,
a book like this always has a way
of soothing the nerves,
quieting the riotous surf of information
that foams around my waist

even though it never mentions
the silent labors of the poor,
the daydreams of grocers and tailors,
or the faces of men and women alone in single rooms—
even though it never mentions my mother,
now that I think of her again,
who only last year rolled off the edge of the earth
in her electric bed,
in her smooth pink nightgown,
the bones of her fingers interlocked,
her sunken eyes staring upward
beyond all knowledge,
beyond the tiny figures of history,
some in uniform, some not,
marching onto the pages of this incredibly heavy book.

Man Listening to Disc

This is not bad—
ambling along 44th Street
with Sonny Rollins for company,
his music flowing through the soft calipers
of these earphones,

as if he were right beside me
on this clear day in March,
the pavement sparkling with sunlight,
pigeons fluttering off the curb,
nodding over a profusion of bread crumbs.

In fact, I would say
my delight at being suffused
with phrases from his saxophone—
some like honey, some like vinegar—
is surpassed only by my gratitude

to Tommy Potter for taking the time
to join us on this breezy afternoon
with his most unwieldy bass
and to the esteemed Arthur Taylor
who is somehow managing to navigate

this crowd with his cumbersome drums.
And I bow deeply to Thelonious Monk
for figuring out a way
to motorize—or whatever—his huge piano
so he could be with us today.

The music is loud yet so confidential
I cannot help feeling even more
like the center of the universe
than usual as I walk along to a rapid
little version of "The Way You Look Tonight,"

and all I can say to my fellow pedestrians,
to the woman in the white sweater,
the man in the tan raincoat and the heavy glasses,
who mistake themselves for the center of the universe—
all I can say is watch your step

because the five of us, instruments and all,
are about to angle over
to the south side of the street
and then, in our own tightly knit way,
turn the corner at Sixth Avenue.

And if any of you are curious
about where this aggregation,
this whole battery-powered crew,
is headed, let us just say
that the real center of the universe,

the only true point of view,
is full of the hope that he,
the hub of the cosmos
with his hair blown sideways,
will eventually make it all the way downtown.

Scotland

It was a weekday afternoon, around three,
the hour some drinkers call the Demon,
and I was possessed by the feeling

that nothing had really changed for me
since childhood,
that I was spinning my wheels in a sandbox,

or let's say that I had been pedaling
around Scotland since 1941,
on the same maroon 3-speed Raleigh bicycle—

that I had begun my life
with clips on my trousers,
pushing off by the side of a garage,

throwing a leg over the crossbar,
then crunching down a straight gravel path.
And now, near the end of the century,

I was still moving over the same
wind-shocked hills, dotted with sheep,
and my terrier curled on a tartan blanket

in my large wicker carrier basket.
I have done all my pedaling in silence,
except whenever I came to an intersection—

a birthday, a wedding, a death—
and then I would ring the bell on the handlebar.
Otherwise, I kept my thoughts to myself,

thoughts of rhetoric and the physical sciences
whenever I had to strain uphill
bending under a stiff wind,

and when I reached a rise and coasted down,
I thought of nothing
but the encrofted cows, and the low hovering clouds.

God knows what I must look like by now,
my shoulders slumped,
my face saying the end of the world is coming,

which it will soon enough for me,
bringing all my pedaling to a close,
easing the pressure of my thumb on the silvery bell.

Then I will dismount, swinging
a leg over the crossbar, standing on one pedal
while the bike slows to a stop

and falls over on its side with me under it,
all the traffic whizzing by
and a woman in a drab raincoat walking over to see.

November

After three days of steady rain—
over two inches said the radio—
I follow the example of monks
who wrote by a window, sunlight on the page.

Five times this morning,
I loaded a wheelbarrow with wood
and steered it down the hill to the house,
and later I will cut down the dead garden

with a clippers and haul the soft pulp
to a grave in the woods,
but now there is only
my sunny page which is like a poem

I am covering with another poem
and the dog asleep on the tiles,
her head in her paws,
her hind legs splayed out like a frog.

How foolish it is to long for childhood,
to want to run in circles in the yard again,
arms outstretched,
pretending to be an airplane.

How senseless to dread whatever lies before us
when, night and day, the boats,
strong as horses in the wind,
come and go,

bringing in the tiny infants
and carrying away the bodies of the dead.

The Iron Bridge

I am standing on a disused iron bridge
that was erected in 1902
according to the iron plaque bolted into a beam,
the year my mother turned one.
Imagine—a mother in her infancy,
and she was a Canadian infant at that,
one of the great infants of the province of Ontario.

But here I am leaning on the rusted railing
looking at the water below,
which is flat and reflective this morning,
sky-blue and streaked with high clouds,
and the more I look at the water,
which is like a talking picture,
the more I think of 1902
when workmen in shirts and caps
riveted this iron bridge together
across a thin channel joining two lakes
where wildflowers now blow along the shore
and pairs of swans float in the leafy coves.

1902—my mother was so tiny
she could have fit into one of those oval
baskets for holding apples,
which her mother could have lined with a soft cloth
and placed on the kitchen table
so she could keep an eye on infant Katherine
while she scrubbed potatoes or shelled a bag of peas,

the way I am keeping an eye on that cormorant
who just broke the glassy surface
and is moving away from me and the bridge,
swiveling his curious head,
slipping out to where the sun rakes the water
and filters through the trees that crowd the shore.

And now he dives,
disappears below the surface,
and while I wait for him to pop up,
I picture him flying underwater with his strange wings,

as I picture you, my tiny mother,
who disappeared last year,
flying somewhere with your strange wings,
your wide eyes, and your heavy wet dress,
kicking deeper down into a lake
with no end or name, some boundless province of water.

The Flight of the Reader

You'd think we would have had enough
of one another
after all the rain streaming down these windows,
the walks out to the garden when it clears,
the same yellow and white flowers,
all the sleepless nights—
the toy car going in circles on the bed table.

But still, you stay perched on my shoulder,
cricket or bluebird,
wild parrot digging your claws into my loud shirt.

Is it because I do not pester you
with the invisible gnats of meaning,
never release the whippets of anxiety from their crates,
or hold up my monstrous mirror,
a thing the size of a playing field?

Whatever makes you stay,
I hate to think of that morning
when I will wake up to find you gone,
heading toward the open sea,
dragging the cables that bound us together,
leaving me with nothing more to say.

But don't get me wrong.
It's not that I cannot live without you,
cannot sit under an ordinary green tree
with no desire to reach for the pen in my pocket,
or lie contented on a couch all day,
one hand over my mouth.

It's not like I have a crush on you
and instead of writing my five-paragraph essay
I am sailing paper airplanes across the room at you—
it's not that I can't wait for the lunch bell
to see your face again.

It's not like that. Not exactly.

This book was set in Perpetua, a typeface designed by the English artist Eric Gill, and cut by the Monotype Corporation between 1928 and 1930. Perpetua is a contemporary face of original design, without any direct historical antecedents. The shapes of the roman letters are derived from the techniques of stonecutting. The larger display sizes are extremely elegant and form a most distinguished series of inscriptional letters.

ALL NEW POEMS
FROM BILLY COLLINS

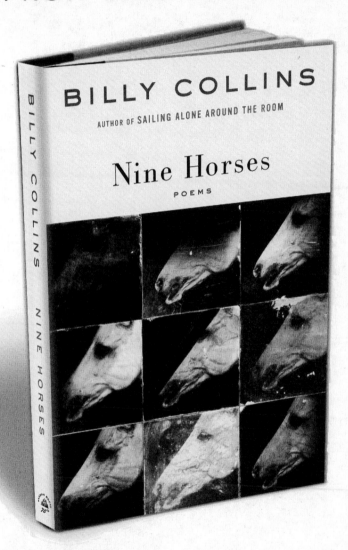

Poet Laureate Billy Collins's first collection of new poems
since the bestselling *Sailing Alone Around the Room*

Now available from Random House